AF225764

Golf Westchester

A Tee to Green
Encyclopedia

DAVE DONELSON

GOLF WESTCHESTER

A Tee To Green Encyclopedia

For information, contact Donelson SDA, Inc.
44 Park Lane, West Harrison, NY 10604

First Edition
ISBN: 978-1-963813-21-0

Photography by John Fortunato and Dave Donelson

Much of the material in this book
appeared originally in

Westchester Magazine
914INC
Hudson Valley Magazine
Met Golfer Magazine
Westchestermagazine.com
Dave Donelson Tee To Green

In memory of

RALPH MARTINELLI

who made it all possible

Praise for Golf Westchester

"Westchester County has some of the finest golf clubs found anywhere in the country. Dave Donelson has been writing about these courses for decades. His insight and knowledge are built from research and relationships he has developed through the years. We are fortunate to read his articles highlighting the unique place Westchester holds in this great game."

-- Carl Alexander, PGA, Director of Golf, Golf Club of Purchase

"Dave Donelson is a respected golf journalist known for his long-standing coverage of the game. In his book, he shares behind-the-scenes stories and insights from years spent covering tournaments, players, and the evolving golf landscape. Drawing on his work with multiple media outlets, Dave captures both the traditions and the modern changes within the sport. During my 43 years as Head Golf Professional at Ardsley Country Club, Dave has become a close friend while thoughtfully capturing and sharing the rich history of the club."

-- Jim Bender, PGA, Head Professional Emeritus, Ardsley Country Club

"Dave has a rare ability to capture what makes golf in Westchester so special, the history, the people, and the traditions that set this area apart. At Salem GC, we've always taken pride in being part of that fabric, and Dave's work reflects a genuine respect for clubs like ours and the role they play in the game. This book is a thoughtful and meaningful tribute to Westchester golf and the community that surrounds it."

-- Joel S. Berman, Salem GC

"We are truly fortunate to be surrounded by some of the oldest and finest golf courses in the United States, both public and private. For decades, Dave Donelson has been one of the leading voices telling the story of the history, the game, and the personalities that have shaped this remarkable golf community. Through his work, he has preserved its rich history, celebrated its traditions, and ensured that the voices and moments that define this special place will endure for generations to come."

-- Greg Bisconti, PGA, Head Professional, The Saint Andrew's Golf Club

"Westchester offers some of the finest golf in the country, with championship-level layouts, historic clubs, and a level of course design that stands out even among the most respected golfing regions. Few writers have captured that excellence as thoroughly as Dave Donelson. His insights have helped shape how golfers understand and appreciate the depth and quality of the game in Westchester."

-- Derek Buckley, CCM, PGA, General Manager/COO Hudson National GC

"Dave Donelson has been a friend and huge supporter of golf in Westchester and the Met area. As a lifelong metropolitan area player and 40 years in Westchester as a PGA Professional, I have witnessed the quality of his work and love of the sport and area. He always has his finger on the pulse and portrays an accurate and positive view of our sport in the county. His words capture the best of golf!"

-- Mike Diffley, PGA, Director of Golf, Pelham Country Club

"No one is more qualified than Dave Donelson to tell the stories of golf in Westchester! Dave is and has been a central figure in golf for many years and his book is a must read for golfers all over the world."

-- Phil Eyre, PGA, Director of Golf, Hollow Brook GC

"Westchester County's golf landscape rivals any across America. Dave Donelson knows it as well as anyone. Dave's tour of these courses, from golden age classics to well-trod munis, speaks not only to his expertise but to his love for how they shine. It should be on the bookshelf of anyone who has had the privilege of sticking a tee into this hallowed ground."

-- Hank Gola, President Metropolitan Golf Writers Association, *Author of Ryder Cup Rivals: The Fiercest Battles for Golf's Holy Grail*

"Westchester has long been a cornerstone of golf in America, and Dave Donelson brings its rich history and unique character to life with clarity and passion. Golf Westchester is a wonderful celebration of a region that has meant so much to the game—and to so many of us who love it."

-- Ann Liguori, Host of Talking Golf and Sports Innerview, Author of *Life on the Green, Lessons & Wisdom from Legends of Golf*

"Golf in Westchester County NY is Dave Donelson's turf! For decades he has chronicled the historic and rich history of Westchester golf. Dave Donelson's 'labor of love' will reward you with a fabulous read."

-- Nelson Long, Jr., PGA Life Member, Metropolitan PGA Hall of Fame

"Dave Donelson is synonymous with Westchester County golf. For decades, he has worked tirelessly to research and highlight the clubs, members, and professionals that make this region one of the most prestigious in the world of golf. Dave has been our greatest advocate and is uniquely qualified to tell our story."

-- James Ondo, PGA, Head Professional, The Apawamis Club

"I have been fortunate to work up and down the East Coast, and nowhere have I fallen more in love with the game than here in Westchester County. Dave has a unique ability to bring that to life, showcasing the wonderful courses, people, and history that make this area so special."

-- A.J. Sikula, PGA, Director of Golf, Sleepy Hollow CC

"The Metropolitan Section and more specifically the Westchester County area has been my home for what is now a 37 year career. Throughout that entire time Dave Donelson has been writing about golf and life in the Westchester area. I look forward to seeing Dave on his visits to Metropolis, as well as reading whatever he puts to pen."

-- Craig Thomas, PGA, 2024 VGA National Champion, Head Professional Metropolis

"Westchester is the envy of golfers world-wide. It's the home of many of America's first—and finest—courses, legendary championships, and a hotbed for emerging talent. Telling golf's 'story' is important and few do it as well as Dave Donelson."

-- Gene Westmoreland, MGA Senior Director Rules & Competitions (1980-2009)

ACKNOWLEDGMENTS

This book would not have been possible without the hospitality and generous cooperation of the many wonderful golf clubs in Westchester County, New York. Their golf professionals, management, and above all, their members, made me welcome time and time again.

I also owe a great debt of gratitude to the Metropolitan Golf Association (MGA), the Metropolitan Section of the PGA of America, and the Women's Metropolitan Golf Association (WMGA) for their support of my efforts.

My partner in crime for most of these last 20 years has been photographer *par excellence* John Fortunato, whose talent and professionalism can be seen throughout this book where his photos are marked (JF).

While I consulted many sources for background information, two that were invaluable were *Golf Clubs of the MGA* and *Under the Apple Tree: The History of Golf in Westchester County,* both written by Dr. William Quirin, my predecessor as official historian of the MGA.

Finally, I must thank Today Media's *Westchester Magazine* and *914INC* and the MGA's *Met Golfer Magazine* for providing a showcase for my work.

CONTENTS

FOREWORD
BRIAN CROWELL, PGA MASTER PROFESSIONAL
2026 NATIONAL PGA PROFESSIONAL OF THE YEAR

It was 1991 when I accepted my first job in the golf business. I joined the staff at Leewood Golf Club in Eastchester as a second assistant golf professional. My wife and I moved to a small apartment in Port Chester with absolutely no clue of where golf would take us. Well, it's been quite a trip. From Leewood, my career led us north to Sleepy Hollow CC and west to GlenArbor GC among other stops. I've worked at great facilities beyond the county borders including Silo Ridge Field Club in upper Dutchess and my current "office" south of the border is Bally's Golf Links at Ferry Point in the Bronx. But in both of those cases the commute has been from Katonah. Since 1991, "home" has always been Westchester County.

This county is also home to world-class golf. As you make your way through this book you'll discover the elite list of clubs that are sprinkled across Westchester. You'll find majestic private courses and classic public-access layouts that were born more than a century ago. You'll gain appreciation for legendary golf course architects, PGA club professionals, even iconic major champions who have made their mark in Westchester County. Do the names Walter Hagen, Gene Sarazen and Ben Hogan ring a bell? How about Tommy Armour, Dave Marr, Claude Harmon or Byron Nelson? Well, at some point each one of them called Westchester County home. Westchester is the birthplace of American Golf (see the chapter on The Saint Andrew's Club in Hastings) and of the PGA Championship (check it out in the chapter on Siwanoy CC in Bronxville). Countless professional tour events and major championships have been decided on Westchester soil . . . and the amateur history in our area is every bit as rich.

To put it bluntly, in terms of golf history and tradition in the United States of America, this county is unrivaled.

The following pages celebrate innumerable stories in golf. Dave Donelson is uniquely qualified to tell those stories. Yes, he's had the privilege of playing each track, but more importantly, Dave is always invited back. In golf he's an amateur, but as a journalist he's a seasoned professional . . . and he's a true gentleman in both arenas. His demeanor is as smooth as his golf swing and no one is more thorough and prepared for an assignment. Dave's passion for golf, Westchester County, and the communities and causes within it is unmatched. His words come from the heart, and what you're about to read is truly a labor of love.

As a PGA Professional, I may be biased, but I insist that golf is the best sport in the world. There is no better network and no game better suited to prepare us for the game of life. Golf teaches patience, it rewards hard work, it introduces us to incredible people and it leads us to some of the most beautiful and peaceful places on earth...many of them right here in Westchester County. This book is a virtual buddy trip to every track our county offers. Put down your phone and enjoy the ride. Enjoy the read. And make more time to enjoy this great game of golf.

INTRODUCTION

Have you ever wondered what really goes on behind the classic stone pillars and imposing iron gates of the world's premier golf and country clubs? I spent the last twenty years exploring those fine places in Westchester County, NY, and I am here to tell you that they are every bit as wonderful as you imagine them to be. The members are more welcoming than you might think, the staff members are professional in every sense of the word, and the facilities—especially the golf courses—set the worldwide standard for excellence.

The first golf I played in Westchester was not at one of those exclusive private clubs, however. It was at Saxon Woods, one of the six public golf courses owned and operated by the county government. I discovered the course in 1979, a time when you slept in your car the night before you played so you could sign up for a tee time the following week because there was no such thing as an online reservation system. Or an online anything, in fact. As I recall, the greens fees were $12. I made many good friends at the course and still play it several times each year, although rather than sleep in my car, I just show up at the crack of dawn and trust the starter to find a place in a group for me. I now qualify for senior rates and play only on weekdays, so I lay out $26 for the privilege. And because I'm playing with other dew-sweepers, a round is well under four hours. What's not to like?

But my golf world exploded like a supernova two decades ago when an editor who knew I played the game asked me if I'd like to attend a meeting about a special golf issue that *Westchester Magazine* was launching. I'd been a freelance writer for quite some time and wrote about many subjects for them and other publications. The magazine, as you may know, is a tremendously successful monthly lifestyle periodical that is a must-read for the million-plus residents of the county. It's the go-to source for information about restaurants, real estate, entertainment, travel, and everything that appeals to readers likely to be club members and golfers. Curious and eager, I accepted the invitation. It was there that I met Ralph Martinelli, publisher of the magazine and an avid, avid golfer.

He liked the editorial ideas I suggested and a beautiful friendship was born.

Since that meeting, I've had the incredible assignment to report on golf in Westchester. My job is to give the readers info they need to enjoy the game, be it by playing better, discovering new places to play, or learning more about the fascinating history of the game. I am not a sportswriter and I don't cover the PGA Tour or USGA Championships unless they're being contested in Westchester, which they occasionally are! Rather, my beat is the Mittelmark Invitational at Fenway, the lesson tee at GlenArbor, the kids golf camp at Sprain Lake. That's where my readers play golf, so that's what I write about. My work led me to be elected to the board of the Metropolitan Golf Writers Association (MGWA) where I also served as President.

My assignments have opened doors—and tee sheets—for me. I've played both courses at Winged Foot many times, had lunch in the grillroom, and even poked around in the file cabinets in the room above the men's locker room where memorabilia from the club's history is stored. I've browsed the shelves of the library in the 54-room mansion that serves as the clubhouse at Old Oaks and enjoyed lunch with a member in his apartment in Westchester Country Club. I once played a round with architect Gil Hanse and queried him about his renovation at Sleepy Hollow. It's experiences like these that have flavored the club profiles I've written for *Met Golfer Magazine* and led me to become the MGA's historian. You'll find many of those articles in this book along with pieces I published in *Westchester Magazine* and elsewhere.

My goal every year is to play every golf course in the county. Between weather and schedule conflicts, I've never quite accomplished it, but I come very close, usually posting more than fifty rounds on Westchester courses every year. Yes, I know, it's a tough job but someone needs to do it, as everyone says. Believe it or not, though, I do approach it as a job, keeping my eyes and ears open on the course and in the grillroom, locker room, and pro shop. I am a journalist, so I take notes, conduct interviews, and shoot photos before, during, and after my round. In between I hit a few golf balls. That's the main source for the material in this book.

I figure I've played some 18,000 holes of golf in Westchester over the last two decades. It's been a lot of fun, but it was also done with a purpose. Each year, I create a composite course of the "Best 18" holes in the county for *Westchester Magazine*. Each year since 2006, I picked a theme that led me to choose particular holes. One year it might be "Best Risk and Reward Holes" while another would be "The Long and Short of Westchester Golf" which highlighted holes with extremes at both ends of the yardage scale. I made a conscious effort to include holes from nearly all the courses, although with only eighteen in each year's article, that meant only about half of them would be covered in any given year. As you explore this book, you'll find nearly every chapter has a section about "Notable Holes" that came from that process.

You'll also notice that the book is organized alphabetically by club name and each piece is dated by when it was first published in print or online. Please note that there may be what seem to be errors like quoting a pro at one club but then quoting someone else in that position in the next article. The dates explain such discrepancies stemming from things like career changes and even changes in club ownership and name. I also did my best to accurately report hole numbers that changed when the courses altered their routing as happened at Anglebrook, Summit, and Pelham. I apologize for any confusion.

Golf in Westchester has been a hugely rewarding part of my life. I hope you enjoy this book as much as I enjoyed the twenty years it took to write it.

I'll be looking for you on the first tee!

Dave

HAPPY BIRTHDAY GOLF
IN AMERICA

Portrait of John Reid in St. Andrew's Club

(2013) If golf can be said to have a birthplace in America, it must be Westchester. Sure, the game was played in a couple of places before John Reid and his buddies whacked a ball around a pasture in Yonkers, but the club they established outlasted them all and built a long, clear path from the beginning of the game to the present day.

Westchester's claim to being the birthplace of golf is based on much more than being home to St. Andrew's, the oldest golf club in America. It was here that the game's national organizations, the USGA and the PGA of America, have their roots. It was here that the first national amateur championship was played, not to mention the first national "Open" tournament that included professionals. It was even here where the dubious tactic of hitting a second ball off the first tee if you didn't like your first one—a Mulligan—got its name.

Westchester is where the greatest golfers of every age, from Harry Vardon and Gene Sarazen to Jack Nicklaus and Tiger Woods, teed it up in the most important tournaments of their day. Where the very best golf architects displayed their artistry. Where the Masters was conceived and the US Open broke Phil Mickelson's heart. If anyplace can lay claim to the honorific, "birthplace of American golf," it is Westchester.

We owe it all to St. Andrew's

It all began when John Reid, a Scottish-born businessman in Yonkers, gathered some friends at a cow pasture on Lake Avenue on a warm February day. His fellow Scot, Robert Lockhart, had brought some hickory-shafted clubs and gutta percha balls back from a business trip to their native land and Reid wanted to show them how to use them. He played an exhibition over three improvised holes with John Upham and golf in Westchester sprouted from there. A blizzard stopped the fun soon after, but when the ground thawed in April, the men moved to a thirty-acre meadow owned by the neighborhood butcher, John Schotts, at North Broadway and Shonnard Place (across the street from St. Michael's Ukrainian Church today) where they could lay out a six-hole course. On November 14, 1888, following some golf and a jolly dinner, Reid, Upham, and three other friends—Henry Tallmadge, Kingman Putnam, and Harry Holbrook, officially formed "St. Andrew's Golf Club of Yonkers-on-the-Hudson." John Reid was elected the club's president.

The minutes of that historic meeting are preserved in the club's archives, the Peter Landau Library, along with a fabulous collection of books, records, and artifacts including early golf clubs and balls. Also in the archives are the minutes of the third meeting, held on March 30, 1889, which report that Mrs. John Reid and John Upham defeated the twosome of Carrie Law and John Reid in a match earlier that day. Even in its infancy, golf in Westchester was far from a men's-only pastime.

By 1892, the jolly crew had moved four blocks north on Palisades Avenue to an orchard where they laid out a new course with an apple tree next to the first tee. It was a great place to hang their coats, not to mention a wicker basket with snacks and libations. Amused passersby soon started referring to them as "The Apple Tree Gang."

Increasing membership and the evolving standards of the game led the club to move to Grey Oaks on the Saw Mill River, a larger property where they could build a nine-hole course. It was there that the first National Amateur Tournament was held in October, 1894, when L.B. Stoddard of St. Andrew's defeated Charles B. Macdonald of Chicago, one of the best golfers of the time and later known as the father of golf course architecture (he designed Sleepy Hollow Country Club's courses among many other great tracks). His loss prompted Macdonald to denounce the championship because it wasn't run by a national organization, so later that year, St. Andrew's secretary and founding member Henry Tallmadge invited representatives of four other leading clubs, the Chicago Golf Club, Shinnecock Hills, Newport (Rhode Island) Country Club, and the Country Club of Brookline, Massachusetts, to dinner at the Calumet Club in New York City. Together, they formed the United States Golf Association and named Tallmadge its first secretary. Macdonald was elected Vice President and walked away happy. The first USGA-sanctioned US Amateur Championship was held the next year at Newport CC and he won handily.

St. Andrew's also hosted the first US Open—at least that's what it was called at the time—concurrent with the National Amateur Tournament. Four top professional golfers of the day were invited to play a competition of their own on the course with a first prize gold medal and $100 going to the champion. That turned out to be Willie Dunn, the pro at Shinnecock Hills, who also designed the original Ardsley Casino course (now Ardsley Country Club) and became its first club pro when it opened in 1896.

"The clubs in Westchester County have played a huge role in the game. Going back to St. Andrew's, so many of the significant and influential clubs here helped start the game. After the USGA, the MGA is the second oldest golf organization in the country. We were originally organized to manage tournaments in the area and, prior to World War II, the Met Open was considered a 'major' around the country. The MGA had a leadership role in development of the handicap system later adopted and expanded by the USGA."

--Jay Mottola, Executive Director,
Metropolitan Golf Association

Golf and St. Andrew's continued to grow. In 1897, the club purchased new property where it could build an eighteen-hole course at Mt. Hope, where it remains today. Members at the time included steel mogul and philanthropist Andrew Carnegie and architect and bon vivant Stanford White. The course was redesigned by Jack Nicklaus in 1985.

While St. Andrew's may have hosted the nation's first mixed foursome, like most golf clubs it wasn't a particularly hospitable place for women. In 1895, John Reid's wife, Elizabeth, and several other St. Andrew's women leased land on North Broadway and established Saegkill Country Club. It soon moved to a site overlooking the Hudson River and by 1896 had 100 members—mostly women. The club also earned a distinctive place in Westchester golf history in 1901 when Benjamin Adams was arrested for playing golf on the course on a Sunday. In a raucous trial, the prosecution lost the case on a narrow interpretation of the statute forbidding disturbance of "the peace of the day," thus establishing every Yonkers golfer's legal right to pursue par whenever he or she chooses.

Golf spreads across Westchester

By the time St. Andrew's started hosting tournaments, a handful of other Westchester clubs were in their nascent stages. John Archbold, John D. Rockefeller's chief lieutenant in Standard Oil, was the first president of Knollwood Country Club, which organized in 1894 on grounds developed by NY attorney Augustus Gillender in Elmsford. Member Lawrence Van Etten, a prominent civil engineer who designed many residential communities in New Rochelle and later the original course at Wykagyl, laid out the first eighteen holes at Knollwood, a par 69 test at 5,305 yards. Seth Raynor designed a longer course that opened in 1925 and features a nineteenth hole that not only takes players back to the clubhouse at the end of their round but serves as a perfect way to settle wagers.

Knollwood was a nationally-known tournament site in the early days of the game. Arthur Fenn from Aiken, Georgia, who later became the first American-born golf professional, won two invitational tournaments there in 1897. Francis Ouimet, winner of the milestone US Open of 1913, played at Knollwood as did the legendary Bobby Jones, who at one time held the course record with a round of 68. It was at Knollwood that Jones met club member Clifford Roberts who, according to local lore, proposed the creation of Augusta National and The Masters Tournament to Jones in the Knollwood grill room.

Willie and Mike Turnesa, two of seven brothers who made an indelible mark on Westchester golf, were affiliated with Knollwood as both amateurs and professionals. Willie was a multiple US and British Amateur winner, captain of the US Walker Cup team, and president of the Metropolitan Golf Association. Brother Mike came to Knollwood as head pro in 1943 after playing on tour for eighteen years. He played in the inaugural Masters Tournament in 1934 and finished second in the PGA Championship to Ben Hogan in 1948.

The first Westchester club to stage a fully-recognized national championship was Ardsley Country Club, which hosted the third US Women's Amateur in 1898. The club had been established in 1895 on the banks of the Hudson River as the Ardsley Casino by Jay Gould, Cornelius Vanderbilt, J. Pierpont Morgan, William Rockefeller, and other notables of the Gilded Age. They had not only an opulent clubhouse but a yacht basin with private dock and their own railroad depot as well, not to mention a golf course built by two hundred men and fifty teams of horses. The Casino was razed in 1936 and the club not only changed its name but moved its clubhouse to its present location, the former home of Frank Jay Gould, in 1966. The course also moved inland from the river and was revised by Donald Ross, Alister MacKenzie, and Robert Trent Jones, Sr., at various times.

Apawamis in Rye began as a social club in 1890, but added a rudimentary nine-hole golf course in 1896. Three years later, it moved to its present location and built an eighteen-hole course that Ben Hogan once called, "the toughest short course I have ever played." The club hosts one of the longest-running golf events in America, the US Senior Golf Association annual championship, which started there in 1905. Apawamis was also the original home of the PGA Tour's Westchester Classic, which began as a one-day pro-am to benefit United Hospital in Port Chester in 1952. The club's history includes two notable caddies, Ed Sullivan and Gene Sarazen, who looped there together in the early 1900s.

Professional golfers make their mark

The PGA of America, with 27,000 members today, has strong ties to several early clubs in Westchester. The organization was founded in 1916, a time when professional golfers lacked the social status of the amateur players of the day. Robert White, a club pro and entrepreneur at Wykagyl Country Club in New Rochelle, became the PGA's first president at a meeting of leading pros and amateurs called by Rodman Wanamaker, son of the department store founder, to organize the group.

Wykagyl was founded in 1898 as the Pelham Country Club, but moved to New Rochelle in 1904 and changed its name accordingly. White came there in 1914 and served as head pro from 1922 to 1927. He was preceded by Horace Rawlins, winner of the first official US Open in 1895. The club hosted the first Met Open to be held in Westchester in 1909, an event considered a major tournament at the time. It is also considered the home of the Westchester Golf Association, which was founded in 1916, and today provides more than a million dollars in college scholarships on a need basis to caddies every year. Wykagyl was noted nationally as a longtime host of LPGA events beginning with the 1976 "Girl Talk" Tournament and ending with the HSBC World Match Play Championship in 2007.

The PGA held its first championship at Siwanoy Country Club, which was founded in 1900 by a group of golfers who played on a nine-hole course in Tuckahoe they reached by trolley. In subsequent years, the club moved closer to home to different locations in Mount Vernon until it settled on the current site in 1913. Donald Ross designed the 18 hole course that saw "Long Jim" Barnes win the first PGA Championship in a final match over Jock Hutchinson in 1916. His prize was $500 and the Wanamaker trophy, which had been donated by Rodman Wanamaker.

> *"Westchester is the cradle of American golf. From the PGA's standpoint, we look at Westchester as being the birthplace of the association. If you look at the first Masters, in 1934, there were ten guys from Westchester clubs in that tournament. The great players of the 40s and 50s were local club professionals like Claude Harmon, Paul Runyon, and Harry Cooper."*
> *--Charles Robson, Executive Director, Metropolitan Section PGA*

The second PGA Championship in Westchester was held at Pelham Country Club in 1923. It was won by Gene Sarazen, a Harrison native and Westchester's greatest home-grown golfer, who had won both the PGA and the US Open the year before. Sarazen, born Eugenio Saraceni, was a major rival of Bobby Jones and Walter Hagen and is one of only five golfers to win all four majors in his lifetime (the others are Ben Hogan, Gary Player, Jack Nicklaus, and Tiger Woods). He won 39 times on tour. Hall of Fame record aside, golfers around the world owe Gene

Sarazen a big debt of gratitude for his invention in 1932 of the modern sand wedge.

Golf gleams in Westchester's Gilded Age

Sleepy Hollow Country Club was founded in 1911 by some of the nation's most prominent business leaders at the pinnacle of America's "Gilded Age." The founding members included John Jacob Astor (who died a year later on the Titanic), William Rockefeller (brother of John D. Rockefeller), and Frank Vanderlip (President of the National City Bank of New York, the forerunner of today's Citigroup). Vanderlip was the creator of the club, which he founded on property he bought from Rockefeller, who had himself purchased it from Margaret Louisa Vanderbilt

Shepard, a granddaughter of Cornelius Vanderbilt.

Charles B. Macdonald, assisted by Seth Raynor, designed the golf course, which was later tweaked by A.W. Tillinghast. The Senior PGA Tour (now the Champions Tour) made Sleepy Hollow a regular stop from 1986-1993. The Sleepy Hollow clubhouse is as magnificent as the golf course. It was completed in 1895 at a cost of $850,000--a huge sum for the time--and retains today the original character and features of the design by architects McKim, Mead, and White. The 75-room mansion includes a ballroom, library, formal dining room, and 18 guest rooms as well as the golf pro shop and locker rooms. An original Tiffany window lights its grand staircase and the view of the Hudson River may well be the finest in the county.

Quaker Ridge Golf Club in Scarsdale is perhaps the best golf course in Westchester to never host a modern major tournament, although it did stage the 1997 Walker Cup. A.W. Tillinghast was commissioned in 1916 to create the course on property where the British army camped in 1776 before defeating George Washington in the Battle of White Plains. The club opened in 1918 and soon became the home of numerous luminaries of the time including Louis Gimbel and Samuel Bloomingdale of department store fame along with composer George Gershwin, who sported a ten handicap. The club has hosted three Met Opens, including the 1935 edition when a young assistant club pro from New Jersey named

Byron Nelson beat the game's top players to begin his legendary professional career. Quaker Ridge is the home of the Hochster Memorial, one of the most prestigious amateur invitational tournaments in the metropolitan area, held to honor William Rice Hochster, the club's first president who lived near the first hole and was known to offer corrective lessons in golf etiquette when he observed infractions.

There were pioneering clubs throughout Westchester. The Bedford Tennis Club added golf in 1891, Scarsdale Country Club opened in 1898, Waccabuc in 1912, and Blind Brook, where President Dwight Eisenhower was a member, was built in 1915.

Golf roars along with the twenties

The Roaring Twenties saw a burst of golf course creation in Westchester that further cemented the county's place in the annals of the game. Westchester Country Club and Winged Foot Golf Club opened in 1922 and 1923 respectively, preceded in 1921 by Bonnie Briar in Larchmont, where artist Norman Rockwell was a charter member and Delmonico's managed the kitchen. Leewood opened in 1922 in Eastchester. Filmmaker D.W. Griffith was a founding member and Babe Ruth joined soon after. A persistent legend has it that the tunnel under the Metro North tracks near the club entrance was built to accommodate the Babe's dash to Yankee Stadium on game days.

Metropolis Country Club in White Plains was established in 1922 and became the home of head pros with admirable records as playing professionals. Paul Runyon, aka "Little Poison," won two PGA Championships while serving as head pro from 1931-1943. Jack Burke, Jr., was head pro for two years before he left to play on tour full time where he won both the Masters and the PGA. "Lighthorse Harry" Cooper won 31 times on tour before joining Metropolis as head pro from 1953-1978. Gene Borek, a Yonkers native who served as Metropolis head pro for 25 years before retiring in 1980, played in eleven PGA Championships and ten US Opens, and was one of the most respected professionals in the game. The current head pro at Metropolis, Craig Thomas, broke the competitive course record at Bethpage Black during the 2007 NY State Open.

Fenway Golf Club opened in 1922 in Scarsdale with 27 holes designed by Devereux Emmet, who also laid out Bonnie Briar, Leewood, Bedford, Rye, Hampshire, and Lake Isle. The members weren't happy with the way their course compared to nearby Winged Foot, however, so they retained A.W. Tillinghast to create a new layout. The course has seen numerous important competitions, but none bigger than the Westchester

108, a six-round event with the richest purse on tour in 1938—a magnificent $13,500. Sam Snead took the $5,000 first prize, beating out soon-to-be greats Byron Nelson and Ben Hogan among others.

You could assign Century Country Club in Purchase to the earliest dates of Westchester golf history, since it was originally organized in 1898 in the Throgs Neck section of the Bronx. It moved to Westchester in 1904 on the site currently occupied by Metropolis, then to Purchase in 1922. Regardless of the decade, the club has been home to several players who made their marks on the game, including one Ben Hogan, who was an assistant pro at Century. Hogan won the Westchester Open in 1940. J.C. Snead, nephew of Sam Snead and eight-time winner on the PGA Tour, was a teaching pro at Century from 1964-1967.

Adjacent to Century in Purchase is Old Oaks Country Club, which began as the Progress Country Club and went through several iterations until merging with the Oak Ridge Club of Tuckahoe in 1936. Willie MacFarlane, winner of the 1925 US Open, was Old Oak's first head pro. Many of the early members were from the entertainment industry and included Albert Warner of Warner Bros. and Moe Gale, who ran the William Morris talent agency. The original course had 27 holes, but the club lost nine of them when I-684 was built.

Nothing is so permanent as change, as someone once said, and that certainly applies to golf in Westchester. Two clubs, Mount Kisco and Willow Ridge, exemplify the way golf clubs have evolved in changing economic and social conditions. The original Mount Kisco Golf Club opened in 1917 on property north of the current course. In 1926, another course was built to serve Lawrence Farms, a residential community. When Mount Kisco Golf Club closed during World War II, many of the members joined Lawrence Farms Country Club and the club became today's Mount Kisco Country Club. Willow Ridge underwent even more transformations. It was built in 1917 by disgruntled members of Apawamis, but closed during the Great Depression. A public course and two private ventures followed (and failed) until, in 1965, the current club was founded.

The 1920s is also when most of Westchester County's public courses were built. The first was Mohansic in Yorktown, which opened in 1925 on land deeded to the County by NY State. Maple Moor in White Plains was acquired in 1925. It was a private nine-hole course that the county expanded to eighteen holes and opened in 1927. Third came Sprain Lake in Yonkers, which was opened in 1929. Saxon Woods in White Plains was added in 1931. Tom Winton, official golf architect for the County parks Commission, designed the four courses (along with Mount Kisco and several other area courses), although A.W. Tillinghast claimed to have been the original designer for Saxon Woods. The fifth county course, Dunwoodie, is actually the oldest, having been established in 1906 as a private club that claimed Mary Pickford and Douglas Fairbanks, Jr., as members. The club stumbled financially, however, and the county bought it in 1955, made substantial improvements, and opened it to the public in 1957.

The county's sixth owned-and-operated course, Hudson Hills, was built on the site of Sunset Hills, a course opened in New Castle in 1926. The club closed during the Great Depression, but was acquired by a group of African-Americans and re-opened as the Rising Sun Golf Club in 1937. It struggled under several different ownership groups until it finally closed in 1982 and the property was sold for development. The county acquired it from IBM and opened the new course in 2004.

The Great Depression and World War II took a toll on the growth of golf everywhere, but the game in Westchester fully recovered. By the 1960s, five new clubs had sprung up (Hampshire, Brynwood, Brae Burn, Rye, and Salem) and two more (Somers Pointe and Lake Isle) were added in the 1970s. A number of truly spectacular courses have opened in Westchester in the last two decades. Hudson National, the Golf Club of Purchase, Trump National Westminster, and Anglebrook burst on the scene in the 1990s, followed soon after by GlenArbor, Hollow Brook, and, in 2008, the county's premiere daily fee course, the Pete Dye-designed Pound Ridge Golf Club.

MGA Historian Dr. William Quirin wrote, "Westchester golfers have been blessed by the convergence of hilly, forested terrain and the genius of visionary golf course architects who created a roster of courses unequaled in the United States." We couldn't agree more.

ANGLEBROOK GOLF CLUB
LINCOLNDALE

Anglebrook clubhouse designed by A.M. Stern (JF)

Because I've played them all many times over the last twenty years, I am often asked to name my favorite golf course in Westchester. I never hesitate to answer, "Anglebrook." It may not be the "best" course—whatever that means—nor is it the hardest, most scenic, or most historic. But it's challenging both physically and mentally and it's always in excellent condition. In other words, I like to play the course and it generally likes me.

The club opened in June, 1997, following nearly a decade of planning, legal hassles, and construction by Kajima USA, the development company that owns and operates it. The course was the last official design of Robert Trent Jones, Sr., often referred to as the father of modern golf course design. Roger Rulewich was the lead architect on the project and the clubhouse was the first one designed by world-renowned architect Robert A.M. Stern.

The course stretches over an expansive 240-acre site that Rulewich used well, routing around and over several protected wetlands that make wonderfully challenging hazards on several holes. There's a really good mix of long and short holes, nearly every one of which requires some strategic thinking. It's not an easy course by any means, but it's playable for a golfer of my mediocre caliber who can usually keep the ball in the fairway and, more importantly, manage his expectations when it comes to carrying hazards. Fairways are generous, but the key to nearly every hole is to drive your ball to the right place to set up your approach. The greens are fast, monstrous large, and strongly contoured, which I love since I'm a pretty fair lag putter.

The nines at Anglebrook were reversed to better accommodate walking golfers during the Covid pandemic. The change also made the opening hole—a short downhill par five—a better way to ease into the round and moved the original controversial round-wrecking eighteenth hole to the ninth position. The change was so popular it was made permanent.

Did I mention the course likes me? My best round in over sixty years of playing this game was at Anglebrook. I didn't break par, but the 74 I shot in a competitive round the year I turned 70 was pretty exciting.

A Memorable Round With Friends (2009)

It has been a difficult weather year for golf, but many of us are still swinging away regardless of the conditions. Yesterday's round at Anglebrook in Lincolndale, NY, proved that if you don't worry too much about your score and play the game for the pure enjoyment of it, you can have a great time regardless of the stuff falling out of the sky. Good companionship helps, which I had with Ralph Wimbish and Dan Berger. Anglebrook GM Matt Sullivan joined us for a few holes, but corporate duties called him back to his desk before things got interesting.

When we started the round, it was cold but dry. A little spitting rain started to fall as we made the turn, but hope springs eternal—especially on the golf course—so we pressed on. The snow didn't really start until the thirteenth hole and by then we were wet anyway, so what difference did it make? Besides, there were only a few more holes to play.

Sixteen (now the seventh hole) at Anglebrook is a short but challenging par five. A fair poke off the tee (250 yards) puts you at the end of the fairway landing area looking downhill to the green 235 yards away. Anything much longer leaves you with a severe downhill lie in the rough, so bombers beware. But from the end of the fairway, you just gotta go for it. Aside from the bunkers, all you have to fear is fear itself, right?

Berger couldn't resist snapping a quick pic with his cell phone and yes, that is snow pelting me as I take my stance and take dead aim at the flagstick on the sixteenth hole. My shot landed just in front of the green and would have made it easily to the putting surface (or so I told everyone within earshot) if the ground had been dry. I attributed my miss of the birdie putt to the weather, too, since at that point in the round I had no feeling in my right hand.

Did I care? Not one whit.

As Wimbish said, "We're playing golf. What do we have to complain about?"

Setting a Record (2022)

As part of the celebration of Anglebrook Golf Club's 125th anniversary, member Masashi Katayama set a new course record for the number of holes played in one day. The intrepid marathoner went around the Lincolndale course four times—each from a different set of tees—in one extraordinary effort. He did it the right way, too, carrying a full set of clubs himself and walking for 72 holes!

Katayama was inspired by the Solstice Club, a 72-hole challenge issued by Bandon Dunes golf resort in Oregon. In this iteration, he teed off at Anglebrook shortly after 6 a.m. and holed his final putt at about 8:30 p.m., a more-than-fourteen-hour endeavor. Various friends and associates accompanied him for some of the rounds. Katayama fueled his marathon with 12 bottles of water, two Gatorades, four rice balls, one banana, and too many energy bars to count. He took 61,239 steps over 24.8 miles. Whew!

The feat generated some fascinating numbers. Katayama reports he took 334 strokes, averaging a score of just over 83 per round. He made four birdies and one eagle and hit 24 greens in regulation. His putter was a big help, especially on Anglebrook's tricky, undulating greens. He took only 122 putts over the four rounds, including 28 one-putts. His longest putt was an improbable 25-foot downhiller on the fifth hole.

The golf course has five sets of tees. The shortest Katayama played from was the 5,597-yard green tees. He started from the tips, which measures 7,001 yards. His next-to-last putt, incidentally, was for a birdie.

Notable Holes

#13, 582 yards, par 5 - (2007) From the looks of it, the environmentally-sensitive hazard that haunts this hole at Anglebrook could be the home of the mythological Bigfoot—and he may be the only player strong enough to reach the hole with fewer than three shots. This par five is the toughest hole on the course and certainly one of the toughest in the county. As Head pro Rob Davis says, "There's no give-up on this hole."

The tee presents a nice wide landing area, although there's a Robert Trent Jones, Sr. signature bunker menacing the left side; Anglebrook was the world-renowned architect's last design and the only course he laid out in Westchester. Just to start you out in the properly intimidated state of mind on this hole, your drive has to fly over an environmentally-sensitive waste area before you get a chance to land in the bunker.

The second shot is the key to the hole—but don't even dream of trying to reach the green. A marshy lateral hazard full of ferns, trees, blackberry brambles, and hundreds of golf balls (and maybe Bigfoot?) hugs the left side of the fairway all the way down, totally blocking your path to the green. "The hole makes a complete 90-degree dogleg," Davis points out. "Your second shot has to get down into the bend inside the 150 marker." That's at least a 200-yard shot for most players. Anything shorter or too far left, and you still can't see—or reach—the green.

When you can finally see the putting surface, you also see the lake in front of it, which you must carry with your third shot. That shot needs to land in the right place, too, because the green is an expansive 48 yards deep with four distinct pockets and a nasty diagonal spine, so three putts—or more—aren't uncommon.

Anglebrook #9 (JF)

#9, 414 yards, par 4 - (2008) Every course needs a round-buster, a hole so hard you know on the tee you're going to have to be either really lucky or really good to make a par, much less a birdie. That's the ninth at Anglebrook, where you can play it safe, safer, or safest—or you can take a big risk and finish your round with one of the most satisfying birdies in Westchester. The key is how you avoid the 25-yard-long bunker that haunts the very middle of the fairway less than 200 yards from the tee.

The safe play is left of the bunker—there's more room there than you think although you're flirting with the environmentally-sensitive waste area if you take that route. Safer is to the right side of the bunker, but that leaves you with a less-than-optimal angle to the green and a long shot to boot. Or you can take the safest play and hit a hybrid off the tee short of the bunker and go for the green with a three wood, the preferred strategy of head pro Rob Davis.

If risk is your thing, though, just go ahead and drive right over the bunker so you have a mid-iron from the perfect angle into the elevated green. Just make sure your drive is no more than 250 yards, however, or you'll end up at the bottom of the waste area that cuts the fairway in two—just one more way this hole can bust your round.

#18, 384 yards, par 4 - (2009) You might put your driver away on this hole, but don't relax, because the finishing hole at Anglebrook simply cannot be taken for granted. It's a prime example of designer Robert Trent

Jones, Sr.'s talent for testing direction and distance control while rewarding two perfectly-struck shots.

Even the straightest of long hitters will need to dial back from the tee because anything hit over 250 yards will disappear into the 50-yard-wide abyss at the end of the fairway. It's a good idea to bite off 240 yards if you can, though, because you'll want to hit as lofted a club as possible into the severe green on the other side of the environmentally-protected waste area. Distance control matters going into the green, too, since putting from above the hole is much like trying to guide a steel ball bearing down the roof of the Chrysler Building into a coffee cup on the sidewalk below.

#10, 425 yards, par 4 - (2017) Robert Trent Jones, Sr., clearly demonstrated his mantra of "hard par and easy bogey" when he created what used to be the first hole on this, his last design. Regardless of philosophy, it may be one of the toughest holes in the county. Two perfect shots—like a 260-yard drive and a high-trajectory 165-yard mid-iron—will give you a possible two-putt par assuming the drive stays out of the fairway bunker on the right and the approach carries the bunkers in front and lands somewhere within shouting distance of the cup on the 12,000 sq. ft. green. A safer play for the second shot is to the alley in front of the right side of the green, which sets up a short pitch or running chip to score a possible one-putt par or pretty much assure a two-putt bogey.

THE APAWAMIS CLUB
RYE

Apawamis Club #1

The Apawamis Club is steeped in history. Since its founding in 1890, Apawamis has hosted championship tournaments on a regular basis and been the home to numerous accomplished golfers. In 1911, Apawamis was the site of the US Amateur, followed the next year by the 1912 Met Open, both considered "majors" in the day. The club has hosted the US Seniors' Golf Association Annual Championship since 1905. It has been home to events including the Curtis Cup, US Senior Women's Amateur, and innumerable MGA and Met PGA tournaments.

Notable golfers that called Apawamis home include Findlay Douglas, the 1898 US Amateur champion and president of the USGA, and Marion "Sis" Choate, the 1963 US Senior Women's Amateur champion and 1974

Curtis Cup Captain. The club's head professional from 1902-1905 was Willie Anderson, who won the US Open four times. Gene Sarazen, the first player to complete the career grand slam, began his career as a caddie at Apawamis.

The current golf course is located on land purchased in part in 1898 from the Charles Park estate (not far from another Park family farm that later became Westchester Country Club). Willie Dunn, fresh from building Shinnecock Hills, laid out the course that pretty much remains today. As would be expected, it evolved for over a century until architect Keith Foster was brought in to return the course to its original concept.

A Ricochet Finish (2015)

Winning at match play depends on skill, talent, grit, and oftentimes a bit of luck. That was certainly true of the first US Amateur played in Westchester, which was held at the Apawamis Club in Rye in 1911.

The US Amateur was a major tournament of the day, second only in importance to the British Amateur, and drew the leading golfers from both sides of the Atlantic. Competing at Apawamis that year were luminaries of the game like Francis Ouimet, Walter Travis, and Charles B. MacDonald.

One of the leading contenders for the Havemeyer Trophy was Harold Hilton, an Englishman who had won both the British Open and Amateur twice by that time. His opponent in the final round, Brooklyn-born Fred Herreshoff, was a lesser light who made a miraculous comeback from six down to tie the 36-hole match and send it into extra holes.

Both players hit good drives on the tricky par four first hole at Apawamis. Hilton played first from the fairway and either shanked or badly sliced his second shot. Luckily (for him) it caromed off a big rock outcropping and landed on the green to set him up for a two-putt par. Apparently, Herreshoff was so unnerved by Hilton's fortunate accident he topped his own second shot, then pitched his third twenty feet past the pin. Hilton two-putted for par to win the hole and the title.

The layout Hilton and Herreshoff played isn't much different from the one members and guests play today, although the course itself has been delightfully updated. Scotsman Willie Dunn laid out the original course in

1896. As with most tracks built in that era, it was modified several times over the years. Gil Hanse authored a renovation/restoration in 2001 and two years ago several new tees were added, bunkers reconfigured, and numerous superfluous (and turf-killing) trees were removed. Apawamis now plays about 300 yards longer, stretching to 6,741 yards.

Notable Holes

#11, 362 yards, par 4 - (2007) According to the course history, Ben Hogan once called Apawamis, "the toughest short golf course I have ever played." When he said it, the tight-lipped Texan may have been referring to the eleventh hole, where two perfect shots are required to make a par and a miss on either one usually means a score worse than a bogey.

Head Pro Jack Perkins says, even though it's a short hole, "You have to hit a good tee shot. If you don't you have to decide whether to lay up or to challenge the hazards in the front and to the left. The green must be approached with a short iron to keep from running through it."

And that tee shot must be straight. "If you hit a draw off the tee, that can mean trouble because the fairway pitches left and there's a lateral hazard there," Perkins explains. Locust Street—definitely out of bounds—awaits the slicer's tee shot to the right. Better players typically hit a three wood or two iron, according to Perkins.

That sets them up for a short iron into the green, but it needs a special touch, too. The green is guarded by a pond on the left, a rock-walled creek in front, and a monstrous trap to the right. Plus, the green is steeply sloped from back to front and toward the water on the left. "If you run through the green, you have a tough pitch coming back down the hill. From the bunker on the right, you're coming back toward the water," Perkins says.

While you're at it, make sure that short iron shot is shaped correctly. "It's best to hit a fade into the green so it will hold the shot," Perkins points out. "A draw brings the water into play."

#14, 446 yards, par 4 - (2011) Golf strategy is seldom dictated so clearly as it is on this long, hard par four. A draw off the tee is essential since anything long and straight—or heaven forbid, a drive that curves right—will put you in the rough with little or no chance to reach the green in two. The second shot is the real killer, though. Most players will be hitting a hybrid or even a fairway wood to carry the ravine and the creek in front of the green. It's essential to fly the ball the full distance, too, since anything short will roll back into disaster. Hit your approach too far, and you'll be in for a probable three-putt (or worse) since the green is steeply canted back to front.

#7, 416 yards, par 4 - (2019) The recent renovation at Apawamis marked a quantum improvement for the venerable club in Rye. Most notable were new bunkers on many holes, extensive tree removal, and some exciting new tee boxes. Easily overlooked, though, is the removal of rough on the hardest hole on the course, the seventh. While you might think it makes the tee shot less risky, the lack of rough actually makes an accurate drive—preferably a long draw—even more important since a fade that's slightly overdone will run and run in the wrong direction on the close-cropped fairway rather than stop in what used to be moderate rough. You will be left with a great lie but a very long approach shot to a green that runs away from the fairway.

#16, 186 yards, par 3 - (2023) An often overlooked but quite valid strategy for this uphill par three is to lay up in front of the green then chip to leave yourself a makeable par putt. The shot is known as a "Patroni" at Apawamis, named for the former head pro who used it consistently to avoid the three deadly misses on the hole—right or left leaves you at best with a bunker shot and at worst with a flop out of long rough, while any shot long and over the green is simply dead on arrival. Of course, you can aim to hit the narrow, sloping green, but what are the odds?

ARDSLEY COUNTRY CLUB
ARDSLEY

Ardsley #1 (JF)

Two hundred men and fifty teams of horses were needed in 1896 to build the first rendition of the course that is today known as Ardsley Country Club. No expense was spared to create a summer playground for Golden Age luminaries including Cornelius Vanderbilt, Jay Gould, J. Pierpont Morgan, and William Rockefeller. Including land, buildings, and the golf course, the cost was $1 million—in 1896 dollars. The club had not only a clubhouse with bedrooms for 60 members but a yacht basin and private railroad depot as well. There were stables that housed 100 horses, including the teams that pulled the Ardsley Tallyho, a "commuter" service that ran each weekday between the club and Hotel Brunswick in Manhattan.

Much has changed since then. The original golf course, designed by Willie Dunn, has been reimagined (and substantially relocated) by architects including Donald Ross, Alister Mackenzie, and Robert Trent Jones, Sr. The former home of Frank Gould was acquired in 1966 to serve as the clubhouse, providing spectacular views of the Hudson River.

A major renovation of the golf course was completed in 2023 under the direction of McDonald Design Group Architect Joel Weiman. It included 86 new or renovated bunkers, 18 new green complexes supported by new irrigation, and redesigns of several fairways.

Notable Holes

#1, 362 yards, par 4 - (2017) One of the most distinctive opening holes in Westchester if not the western world, this short but surprisingly difficult charmer typically befuddles the golfer who encounters it for the first time. "Put the driver away," your caddie will say. "Don't hit anything over 180 yards." It's advice well-taken since the picturesque pond at the end of the fairway begins about 200 yards in a blind spot you can't see from the radically elevated tee box. Assuming your tee shot stays dry, you're then faced with a short iron or wedge over the pond to the small green protected by water on the right and bunkers on the left.

#2, 248 yards, par 3 - (2009) It's tempting to think this monster par three plays shorter than the yardage because it's downhill, but don't fool yourself—it plays the full distance. Par requires accuracy, too, since there is OB and a water hazard to the left and a devilish bunker on the right front. The green itself is huge—44 yards deep—and has more curves than a contortionist at a sideshow audition, so two-putts are anything but guaranteed.

#3, 419 yards, par 4 - (2008) Early in your round at Ardsley, you're faced with a man-sized par four that you can trim down to a make-able birdie opportunity with a long, high draw over the trees on the left. Miss that long drive, though, and you're in trouble—those maples are there for a reason. You'll either be blocked from reaching the green at all with your second shot or have at best a long, long recovery shot. The safe route is the wide fairway to the right, where you'll then face a second shot with a long iron or hybrid. Even that's no guarantee of a par, though, since it's tough to land your approach in just the right position on a green the size of Rhode Island with more curves than a kettle-fried potato chip.

#4, 511 yards, par 5 - (2010) Some of the greatest names in golf architecture had a hand in shaping today's course at Ardsley. The original layout was by Scotsman Willie Dunn in 1895 while Donald Ross reconfigured the course in 1917, followed by Robert Trent Jones in 1965 and Ken Dye in

2005. In 1928, Alister Mackenzie put his imprimatur on several holes, including the classic split-fairway fourth. Long hitters can reach the green in two by driving up the right side, while conservative players can play their tee shots up the middle, lay up to the left of the trees dividing the fairway, and have a short iron to reach the green in regulation. The green itself is Ardsley's toughest. It's only 22 yards deep and has a wicked false front that you must avoid at any cost.

#15 326 yards, par 4 - (2024) One of the best design improvements at Ardsley last year was the reconfiguration of this classic short par four. The green was doubled in size so that now the carpet wraps around the full width behind the pond that keeps big hitters (usually) from driving the green. The new configuration created a daunting new pin position for those who have pinpoint control of their wedges.

BEDFORD GOLF & TENNIS CLUB
BEDFORD

Bedford Golf & Tennis #10

Country casual is the style of Bedford Golf & Tennis Club. The club is a very family-oriented sports club where junior golfers are welcome, as many members walk as ride carts, and the entire vibe is reminiscent of the founding year of 1891.

Devereux Emmet designed the present course in 1927, taking full advantage of the many elevation changes that give the track its character. He also routed the course so that water is in play on six of the first eleven holes.

Notable Holes

#10, 162 yards, par 3 - (2010) Not every golf hole has to be hard to be pleasurable, although the fine par three at the turn at Bedford G&T is no push-over. The hole is a visual feast that you should take a few minutes to enjoy from the elevated tee box before you take your swing. The green is a jewel set in a ring of pristine bunkers flanked by fescue-covered hillsides with seasonal flowers providing colorful highlights and mature maples and oaks a dramatic backdrop. When the air is calm, the entire scene is reflected in the mirror pond that lies between you and the flag.

#7, 392 yards, par 4 - (2019) Every shot you hit on the number one handicap hole at Bedford G&T is tinged with danger. Your tee shot needs to fly 235 yards to reach the dogleg and give you a shot at the green, but 250 and straight will put you through the fairway into the rough leaving a next-to-impossible second shot.

Even from the fairway, you'll need at least one more club and probably two to carry your approach to the tiny green atop the steep hill in front of you. Come up short and you'll be lucky if your ball rolls back and stops in the fairway instead of the thick rough on either side of the narrow approach alley.

#14, 438 yards, par 4 - (2009) The first time I stood on the tee box for this hole, I groaned. The shot was uphill, you couldn't see the landing area, and there was obvious trouble in the form of bunkers right and trees on both sides of that portion of the fairway you could see. The second time, though, I grinned with anticipation, knowing the reward that I would get if I could drive the ball straight and to the top of the hill. As my high school physics teacher pointed out, what goes up must come down—and so it is with the fairway on this medium-length par four. The hill peaks at about 250 yards off the tee, so a good drive will catch the down-slope and run down to short-iron territory. You'll need that help, though, because the elevated green is one of the most difficult on the course, with three tiers and a matching number of ridges running through it. There is also a sprawling bunker complex protecting the left front that you don't want to challenge with a long-iron approach shot.

THE BLIND BROOK CLUB
PURCHASE

In a county filled with upmarket golf clubs, Blind Brook stands alone. Known as the "CEO's" club, it keeps a very low profile that well serves its role as a private place where restful tranquility rules the day. Before Dwight Eisenhower was elected President of the United States, he served as president of Columbia University and was a member of Blind Brook.

The golf course, designed by Seth Raynor to NOT be a championship test of staggering length, is an easy walk among a collection of template holes familiar to followers of Raynor's work. Fairways are generous but the greens are undulating and call for a deft short game.

BONNIE BRIAR COUNTRY CLUB
LARCHMONT

Bonnie Briar #8 (JF)

Golf exploded in Westchester during the Roaring Twenties, a decade when more courses were built in the county than in the previous thirty years—and just about as many as in the ninety years since. Topping the list is Winged Foot Golf Club, founded in 1921. Its two legendary golf courses opened in 1923. Right across the street from Winged Foot, though, another Westchester club was coming into its own at the same time. Bonnie Briar Country Club was founded in 1921 on the estate of Colonel Lyman Bill, a publisher and one of Theodore Roosevelt's Rough Riders. His son, Edward Bill, was the club's first president. A rudimentary course that had been on the property since the 1800s was replaced by a new one designed by Devereux Emmet with contributions from A.W. Tillinghast in 1923. Among the notable Bonnie Briar members over the years were illustrator Norman Rockwell and Masters and PGA champion Doug Ford.

Notable Holes

#13, 458 yards, par 4 - (2010) The number one handicap hole at Bonnie Briar features a smorgasbord of pleasures from the winding Sheldrake River and one of the course's most dramatic rock formations to an elevated tee box and a green with a deceptive false front. Long and straight is a must off the tee, since not only are you driving to a blind landing area, but thick woods encroach on the left side of the fairway while a rock wall lines the right. The second shot is even more of a challenge with the river cutting across the fairway about 60 yards in front of the green and bunkers flanking it on both sides. Long and straight works best here, too, since the green is only about 20 paces wide. Plenty of players lay up to the water and make their par with a wedge.

Bonnie Briar #13 (JF)

#7, 309 yards, par 4 - (2012) This may be one of the shortest par fours on the course, but don't try to drive the green. It's elevated—a lot—and surrounded by thick rough and some nasty bunkers. Watch where you play your conservative iron or hybrid off the tee, too. The landing area slopes right to left and feeds into a fairway bunker just where you don't want it to—about a hundred yards short of the green. Laying up to perfect wedge distance may not be as easy as it sounds.

Perhaps the most unnerving shot on the hole, though, is the one to the green. You can't see the surface from the fairway below. In fact, you may not even see the flag. Unless you have a deep store of local knowledge, take a minute to walk up to the green and find your target. It may add a few minutes to the round, but the jaunt will probably save you a stroke or maybe even two.

#6, 403 yards, par 4 - (2020) Bonnie Briar may be celebrating its centennial this year, but the club hasn't hesitated to update its golf course with major improvements in the modern era. Among the most significant was a restyling of the sixth hole, where a boggy creek was converted to a pretty pond that raises the interest level of the dogleg hole substantially. "Play off the elevated tee as close as you dare to the water on the left," advises head pro Frank Mattei. "If you're accurate, you will have only 150 yards left to the green." The safe play to the center of the fairway will guarantee a dry golf ball but a long, uphill approach.

#8, 408 yards, par 4 - (2025) What looks like a straightforward par four is anything but, according to head pro Joe Condomitti. The best angle to the green will come from a drive placed in a small fairway landing area on the left. It may look safer to hit to the center or right side, but that will leave a near-impossible shot to the green. To drive the ball where you want it to go, Condomitti says, tee the ball high and forward in your stance and don't sway when you swing.

#11, 453 yards, par 4 - (2023) This dogleg right may play downhill, but it's still a long, long journey from tee to green. The best line to the green is from the right side of the fairway, but beware the bunker just off the short grass that's within reach of a solid drive. The second shot is long, too (and blind to boot), but at least the green isn't surrounded by sand. Check your approach line before you swing and aim for the left side of the green, which tilts right.

BRAE BURN COUNTRY CLUB
PURCHASE

Brae Burn #8 (JF)

A group of golfing friends and neighbors got together in 1964 to form Brae Burn Country Club. Spearheading the group was avid golfer and prominent commercial real estate developer of the Platinum Mile along I-287 in Harrison, Lowell Schulman, who had been working on a golf course in Purchase with architect Frank Dunne. The course they created is hilly and forested with brooks and ponds throughout.

Notable Holes

#15, 495 yards, par 5 - (2006) You can let out some steam with a long drive off the tee at this eye-pleasing, downhill par five that features just about every hazard in the book as well as one that isn't, an old railroad trestle abutment that actually comes into play for those afflicted with a slice.

Head professional Paul Alexander says, "Your drive will always put you in the 'go' zone. It's very risk/reward. I've made plenty of threes on it, but I've also made plenty of sevens because the second shot has to be very precise. One thing that encourages the player to go for the green in two is because it looks like such a great, fun shot to hit."

It is fun. All you have to do is avoid the pond guarding the left front of the green, the lateral water hazard to the right, and the punishing bunker on the right front of the green that squeezes the approach and guards a rear right pin location. If you're in that bunker, the green slopes away from you, making it difficult to get up and down. Hit long and you'll end up in one of three bunkers behind the green shooting back toward the water.

As Alexander warns, "If you go for it, it can be very penalizing."

Abandoned railroad trestle on Brae Burn #15

(2026) Most players don't give much thought to anything but whether to lay up or go for the green on this picture-perfect par five. If you pause on your way down the hill and look to your right, though, you will encounter the ghost of a railroad that never ran. Just off the fairway are the remains of a stone trestle built for the never-to-be tracks of the Westchester Northern Railroad Company, a project that died from financial distress long before completion in 1925. If you sight along the line of the trestle, you'll see another manmade knoll across the seventeenth fairway. Beyond that (and out of sight from this hole) is the tee box on #5, which is railroad flat and straight for a reason. Some 23 miles of roadbed were graded for the route by previous aspirants to railroad riches as early as 1863.

#5, 140 yards, par 3 - (2012) The fifth hole at Brae Burn may be a perfect par three. It has a forced carry over water, plenty of sand, a large undulating green, and scenic features like a trickling waterfall and colorful shrubs and flowers that are good for the soul.

Depending on the placement of the tee markers and the pin position on any given day, the hole can play from 120 to 160 yards, so proper club selection is crucial. The three bunkers protecting the green can cause problems, but the real danger is landing your ball above the hole, especially if there is a front pin. You probably won't putt into the water if you stroke it a little strong, but your ball can very easily trickle down the false front and make you pray a little as it heads toward the pond.

#8, 190 yards, par 3 - (2022) The eighth hole at Brae Burn is pretty—pretty deadly, that is. It features a forced carry over water to the green, there are bunkers on both sides, and the green slopes heavily front to back so any ball long leaves you with an impossible downhill recovery shot.

Head pro Nick Yaun says, "There's nothing but trouble on this hole. Quite a few members lay up and that's not just the short hitters. If you're a little wild, it's not a bad play. It leaves you a good chance for a three or at worst a four, and avoids the penalty strokes that kill your score."

#9, 495 yards, par 5 - (2007) All the hazards on this reachable par five are around the green, but they affect your first shot as much as any other. From the tee, the fairway is wide open, level, and invites a big swing. Listen to your caddy, though, when he tells you to drive to the left side of the fairway. Not the center, not the left half, but the left edge. That's the only place that will give you a second shot with any chance of hitting the green.

The major hazard here is a stand of tall, tall, trees blocking the entire green on the right. Unless you have a club in your bag that will shoot the ball straight up and drop it straight back down 250 yards away (aka a howitzer), you can't make the green in two from the right side. The trees—and the bunker behind them—even complicate a lay-up from the right.

The green is canted and protected by two bunkers on each side. If you manage to hit through the green, you end up in the starter's building, which leaves an embarrassing pitch back onto the green.

CENTURY COUNTRY CLUB PURCHASE

Century #18

Century was founded in 1898 as a place "to encourage and stimulate an interest in outdoor sports" for a group of leading NY businessmen. Initially located on a nine-hole course near the Throgs Neck bridge in the Bronx, the club later built eighteen holes in Greenburgh (which now serves Metropolis CC), then in 1923 moved to its current site in Purchase. Charles Alison, partner in Colt, Mackenzie (of Augusta National fame), and Alison designed the course. Over the years, the course has seen extensive changes by Tillinghast, RT Jones, Sr., Gil Hanse, and most recently by Keith Foster, who restored many of the original Alison concepts.

In 1938, the club hired Ben Hogan as an assistant to the original head pro, Dan Mackie. Hogan and his wife, Valerie, lived in an apartment in the clubhouse and he was assured that he would be allowed to play in a few tournaments outside the club. In 1940, Hogan was promoted to head professional, a job he held for another year. During his time at Century, Hogan entered 60 events, made 59 cuts, had 49 top ten finishes, and won five times. He didn't give many lessons to Century members.

Nelson Long, whose father was credited by Sam Snead with teaching him the finer points of competitive golf when they were both on staff at the Homestead in West Virginia, joined Century as an assistant in 1974 and became head pro in 1976. His resume includes a unique bookend accomplishment: he played in two USGA championships 45 years apart, the US Junior in 1968 and the US Senior Open in 2013 at the age of 62.

Since 1960, Century (along with Old Oaks) has hosted the US Open Sectional Qualifying tournament on a three-year rotation.

Notable Holes

#6, 430 yards, par 4 - (2006) Ben Hogan would have enjoyed this hole when he was assistant pro at Century before the second World War. It sets up perfectly for his trademark draw, with a fairway that slopes right to left matching the slight dogleg.

"Two well-struck shots will be rewarded," according to head pro Nelson Long, Jr., "You can make a birdie. Even in perfect position off the tee, you still face a small, well-guarded green," Long advises. "It's going to require a precisely hit iron shot."

There is a large bunker above the green on the right and a huge one below it on the left. The front part of the green also slopes right to left matching the fairway, so even a slight pull is likely to end up in that left bunker. The perfect approach is a slight draw to the right front of the green or even a little short of it, depending on the pin placement.

The hole still plays as it was laid out by architect C.H. Alison in 1926, although there are many more trees, especially on the left side.

#5, 451 yards, par 4 - (2009) Nelson Long has a easy manner of speaking that makes every hole sound like a piece of cake. "Just stay out of the bunker on the right," he drawls when asked about how to play the demanding fifth hole at the club. "Then keep your approach shot to the left side of the green because it all slopes to the right." He's correct, of course, but it's never quite as easy as Long makes it sound. The target from the tee is a beautiful maple tree on the far edge of the fairway over the hill. Anything to the right of that is good (as long as it's in the short grass), but a drive to the left will leave a long, tricky approach. The second shot plays downhill, but don't count on running your approach onto the green; there's a slight swale in front that will leave you short.

#1, 444 yards, par 4 - (2017) What used to be a good opening hole has become a great one with the renovation at Century CC this winter. As part of the club's two-year renovation, architect Keith Foster made one major change and a few minor ones on the hole that simultaneously make it tougher for the big hitter and a little more manageable for the rest of us. The big change was moving the fairway bunker from the right rough to the left and expanding it, taking it out of the landing area for the slice-afflicted player while bringing it perfectly into place for the aggressive golfer trying to play a slight draw. Both players will face the newly-collarless green complex, which gives many more short game options.

#17, 221 yards, par 3 - (2020) Plenty of mid-handicap players use a driver on Century's penultimate hole, one of the longest par threes in the county. It's really a leap of faith, though, to believe you can stop the ball on the green if you need a driver to get there. Depending on the pin position, wind, and the vagaries of their swing, the thinking player may opt to lay up to their favorite wedge distance or even aim for the right side alley to the green where they can bump their second shot to the cup.

DUNWOODIE GOLF CLUB
YONKERS

(2021) Dunwoodie was known as "the golf course of the stars" when it was founded as a private club in 1906. Mary Pickford and Douglas Fairbanks, Jr. were among the many show biz personalities who belonged to the club before the Great Depression ruined its finances. The county acquired it in 1955, spent a princely half million dollars improving it, and opened it to the public two years later.

Dunwoodie is the shortest of the county's six courses and known to be one of the easiest on the handicap. Its location at the top of Dunwoodie Heights in Yonkers dictates some steep slopes and dramatic topography along with many narrow, twisting fairways and small greens that reward deft approaches. Most of the fairways are accessible and few of the holes require a booming drive. Dunwoodie features five par 3s, including the 154-yard seventh hole, with its very fine view of the Manhattan skyline.

Longer hitters will appreciate the seventeenth hole: 419 yards on the scorecard that seem like 450. The green is small and narrow, too, and most pars come from a one-putt left after the player misses the green with the approach shot and chips close to the hole.

FENWAY GOLF CLUB
SCARSDALE

Fenway #13 (JF)

Centennial (2024)

One hundred years ago, the first golf ball was struck on a new course designed by A.W. Tillinghast for Fenway Golf Club. The Scarsdale club observes its centennial this year by "celebrating both the old and the new," according to club president Marc Lisker. The celebration will kick off with a party in June and be marked throughout the year by a special logo everywhere. In the fall, the club will host the Tillinghast Cup, a Ryder Cup-style tournament involving the head pros and club leaders from what the Tillinghast Society considers the top ten courses he designed including Ridgewood, Baltusrol, Winged Foot, Quaker, and Fenway.

Fenway's celebration reflects its eminent stature in Westchester's rich golf community. In 2022, it hosted the 120th Met Amateur and last year it co-hosted its first USGA event, the US Mid-Amateur championship. In the decade prior, the course was renovated under a master plan created by Gil Hanse. Most recently, all the bunkers and bunker faces were redone with the latest technology and tee boxes have been rebuilt and redesigned.

Each spring, Fenway holds the Mittelmark Invitational Tournament where accomplished amateurs are invited to test their games against the course. Many of its champions like Cameron Young have gone on to successful PGA Tour careers. 2015 Champion Stewart Hagestad went on to win the 2016 US-Mid Amateur Championship as well as the 2023 Mid-Am.

Reflecting the changing lifestyles of its members, the club is working with an architectural firm to develop a master plan for club facilities other than the golf course. "We consider ourselves a family," says former president Bruce Frank. "There are many, many members that are multi-generational at the club. We like to operate so that members consider Fenway simply an extension of their home." A new pool and patio have already been built. Among changes under consideration are opening dining rooms for more outdoor experiences and re-designing the racquet sports facility.

One feature the club doesn't want to change is its ambiance. "Fenway is a welcoming place," Lister says. "People socialize, they hang out together. The club's done a great job of increasing the diversity of membership." He adds that the club follows its own path: "We see what other clubs are doing and appreciate them, but we are Fenway and we shape our club to best serve our membership, not compete."

Notable Holes

#18, 520 yards, par 5 - (2006) The last hole is an uphill par five that A.W. Tillinghast designed in 1924 and Gil Hanse restored in 2000 on the old James Fenimore Cooper estate. According to Head Pro Heath Wassem, "It's a hole where you can easily make eagle or double bogey in a breath." The fairway slopes left to right, so your drive has to be a draw in order to finish in the short grass. Then you get to hit a long uphill second shot through a tight, narrow chute of oak trees. If you can avoid four bunkers flanking the 10,000 square foot green, the real fun begins.

The green slopes back to front through two tiers and numerous undulations, making double, triple, or even quadruple breaks the rule of the day. "It makes for some really exciting finishes," according to Wassem.

#14, 435 yards, par 4 - (2007) A.W. Tillinghast, designer *par excellence* of numerous great golf courses in Westchester, was known to partake of the grape; to knock back a few with the boys, as they say. When you approach the array of bunkers he scattered up, down, and around the four-teenth fairway and green at Fenway, you can find that legend easy to believe. They look exactly like something imagined by a golf course designer under the influence of alcoholic hallucinosis. When Gil Hanse refurbished the course in 2000, he made them tougher.

The bunker complex starts a hundred yards from the green. From that point it's nothing but sand, grass, sand, grass, sand, grass—you get the idea. There is one bunker shaped like an angry amoeba, another like a crazed crocodile creeping across the fairway from the right side. On the left is a lion waiting to pounce, or at least a bunker contoured like one. There is more sand beside and behind the green, which itself has more rolling contours than a boa constrictor in a bushel basket.

If you finish this hole in par—with all your limbs intact—you might want to celebrate the feat with a wee dram yourself.

#1, 285 yards, par 4 - (2008) The first hole at Fenway is soooo tempting. The front of the green is only 270 yards from the tee—the center just 285! Head Pro Heath Wassem says for an easy start you should just take a hybrid off the tee to comfortable wedge distance, pitch on for a two-putt-par on the large, rolling green, then go on to the next tee. But why begin your round with a par when you can get a jump on the game with a bird—or even an eagle? Besides, layups are for basketball, aren't they? All you have to do is hit your drive a few extra yards to that huge, inviting green. Pay no attention to the acres of sand surrounding every approach angle, or to the trees on the right waiting to turn a slice into a pitch-out bogey. Just bomb it!

#3, 510 yards, par 5 - (2010) Don't be lulled into complacency by the inviting tee shot on this tame-looking par five. One small slip—an overly aggressive swing that turns into a longer than normal fade, perhaps—and you may find yourself in an ocean of sand scrambling for damage control. The ultimate nightmare, of course, is escaping from one bunker only to hit into another, a prospect that's all too real on your second shot when you consider that the bunker complex on the right side is almost as long as a football field. Even if you stay in the fairway and smash your drive, you're left with an monster approach to a big two-tiered green fronted by 15 yards of rough and guess what?—more bunkers.

#13, 391 yards, par 4 - (2020) Architect Gil Hanse altered just about every feature on this hole to build interest by providing different angles of play. A line of trees in the left rough was removed since they primarily hurt bogey golfers, but a bunker replaced them about 240 yards from the tee to keep the stronger players honest. It pinches the fairway but can be carried by a 280-yard uphill drive. The bunker on the right side of the fairway was moved into play as well. Head pro Tyler Jaramillo adds, "The green complex became a lot more interesting. The potato chip green was expanded and three swales make for some really fun approach shots."

#15 par 4, 305 yards - (2026) Sam Snead made history of several sorts by winning the Westchester 108—a six-round PGA marathon tournament played in 1938 for a purse of $13,500, the largest on the tour that year. Among many other highlights (and lowlights) of the tournament, Slammin' Sammy carded a horrid triple bogey on this testy little hole by blasting from bunker to bunker to bunker in an early round before hitting his ball over the heads of spectators from the fourteenth fairway to birdie the hole during the final round.

GLENARBOR GOLF CLUB
BEDFORD HILLS

GlenArbor #18 (JF)

MGWA Club of the Year (2023)

Established in 2003, GlenArbor Golf Club is one of the youngest of the 42 clubs to be recognized as the MGWA Club of the Year. The club's record of service to the game, however, belies its age.

GlenArbor founder Grant Gregory retained Gary Player to design the golf course and focused the club on a mission with four key pillars: the traditions of golf with an emphasis on camaraderie and friendly competition; continued stewardship of the land as illustrated by its dedication to conservation; a commitment to giving back through charitable partnerships; and a continuous lifetime of learning.

"The Gregory family put their trust in me and my staff to create a unique and environmentally conscious course, that was steeped in tradition and tucked away from distraction," said Hall of Fame champion Gary Player. "I was elated to learn the Metropolitan Golf Writers Association gave GlenArbor the distinguished honor of being named its Club of the Year. Many congratulations to everyone involved that makes this place so special. They are all true stewards of the game we love."

Key to GlenArbor's stature is the golf course that Player describes as "my masterpiece." The legendary champion created a course that emphasizes natural beauty while presenting exciting challenges to golfers of every level. The 7,100-yard track rolls and turns through woodland, wetlands, and dramatic elevation changes that call for both draws and fades, length and finesse. Greens are expansive but demand a keen eye and masterful touch.

In addition to the championship course, a world-class short game teaching facility, also designed by Player, and a state-of-the-art teaching center set the standard for such facilities in the Met area. The club's nationally-recognized staff of PGA professionals, led by PGA Tour Champions competitor Rob Labritz, is dedicated to game improvement for players of all levels. GlenArbor's innovative Prodigy program has produced many competitive young golfers over the years.

The property in Bedford is blessed with unspoiled wetlands, natural glades, and abundant wildlife, all carefully preserved by the club in a manner that was recognized by the MGA Foundation with the 2010 Arthur P. Weber MGA Club Environmental Leaders in Golf Award.

GlenArbor's beautiful and challenging golf course has been the site of numerous MGA championships including the Mid-Amateur championship, as well as professional charity golf events like the annual Berenberg Invitational, which recently raised more than $1.5 million for the University of Nebraska Buffet Cancer Center for the cure of pancreatic cancer. The event draws a pantheon of legends of the game including Tom Watson, Fred Couples, Bernhard Langer, as well as the tournament founder, Gary Player.

The GlenArbor clubhouse was built on the site of the Harold T. White estate, known as "Lakeover." Harold White's wife, Ruth Underhill White, was the 1899 US Ladies Amateur Champion and her trophy is on display in GlenArbor's clubhouse, another demonstration of the club's commitment to permanently protect the property's historic roots. The classic facility, designed by Mark Finlay, looks as though it could have stood sentinel while George Washington's troops marched through the property, yet has all the amenities desired by discerning modern golfers.

Gary Player celebrates GlenArbor's Anniversary (2013)

GlenArbor Golf Club, the premier Westchester club located in Bedford Hills, NY, celebrated its tenth anniversary with a special visitor—golf legend Gary Player. Members, staff, and a few select guests had the opportunity to play and chat with the Black Knight for two memorable days.

Player designed the course, which was built on a spectacular site with a perfect mix of elevation changes, water, and tremendous vistas. He said he recognized the potential for a beautiful golf course the first time he walked the property.

At the reception that topped off Player's visit, he had nothing but good things to say about the GlenArbor staff, who, he said, "Always greet you with a smile." The club also earned his highest praise for its dedication to the game. "This club knows and demonstrates how important the traditions of golf are to the growth and well-being of the game."

Player said he was particularly pleased to see the GlenArbor learning center, which he said he recommended when the course was first built. GlenArbor not only has a practice range (double-ended), but a fully-equipped year-round teaching center with heated hitting bays as well. The real gem is the short game area, which features four practice greens, three target greens, five teeing areas, and every kind of sand trap, grass bunker, long rough, short rough, and greenside fringe the devilish designers could imagine.

In addition to the regular cups, the practice greens also have nine red-flagged holes. These correspond to numbered "tees" arranged off the greens. Together, they make up a nine-hole "course" that is re-routed every day but typically includes two bunker shots, two pitches out of rough, two tight lies, a lag putt, and other tests of your ability to get up and down. There's a par eighteen scorecard, too, and a nearby computer terminal to enter your scores so you can track your progress.

The Gary Player Center, named to honor the course designer, has five teeing grounds surrounding three dedicated greens, each of which has three pin positions, so the player has nine targets at various distances from ten to a hundred yards away. There's a fairway bunker to practice the scariest shot in golf, as well as a sod-faced bunker to get you ready for St. Andrews.

A Unique 19th Hole (2015)

When two creative golf industry professionals like Brian Crowell and Michael Lehrer start brainstorming, spectacular things happen. The latest creation from Crowell, the head professional at GlenArbor Golf Club in Bedford and Lehrer, owner of Home Green Advantage in Armonk, evoked oohs, ahs, and quite a few guffaws of delight when it was unveiled this weekend. It's a near-perfect replica of the club's fourteenth green that floats—yes, floats!—in the middle of the lake below the clubhouse.

"It's the coolest shot in golf," says Crowell of the pitch shot from the patio of the classic GlenArbor clubhouse to the green in the middle of the lake below. "It's the perfect way to settle your bets—or make a few more—

at the end of your round," he points out before adding with a wicked grin, "There's also nothing more satisfying than watching your opponent's ball splash into the lake after yours lands safely on the green." Crowell's light-hearted approach to the game is well known to viewers of the Golf Channel, where he hosted "Lesson Tee Live" earlier this year.

GlenArbor #19 Island Green

Both Knollwood and Wykagyl have nineteenth holes to settle matches, but the floating green is certainly unique to Westchester and possibly the East Coast. Island greens like the famed seventeenth at TPC Sawgrass aren't unusual but nearly all of them, however, actually have a land-bridge of some sort and aren't floating in the water like GlenArbor's.

Lehrer, who has designed and constructed thousands of artificial greens and practice facilities in the metro area, made the 14-by-21-foot green more receptive than normal so that chances of making a successful shot are improved. "I have to admit," he says, "it's one of the more unusual projects we've undertaken. We had a lot of fun with it."

No one seems to know who will be responsible for retrieving balls from the bottom of the lake.

The floating green was the highlight of the Traditions of Golf Invitational, an annual event staged by GlenArbor to thank members of the golf community and media for their contributions to the sport. Honored with the "Traditions of Golf" award this year was Major Dan Rooney, founder of the Folds of Honor, a non-profit that has raised over $70 million for educational scholarships to the family members of soldiers killed or disabled in combat.

Notable Holes

GlenArbor #4 (JF)

#4, 415 yards, par 4 - (2023) The drive determines your likely success on the #1 handicap hole at GlenArbor. Long matters a lot, but straight may matter more since there's trouble both left and right. Head pro David Gagnon says the most important step is the first one you take walking up to the tee box. That's when you should mentally visualize a positive picture of a long, straight drive. "Then just let go," he says, "Forget all those technical swing thoughts and swing free."

#7, 206 yards, par 3 - (2006) At least half the fun of playing this exciting par three is visualizing your shot from the tee. In your mind's eye, your ball sweeps over the valley in a long, arching fade, lands on the front of the canted green left of the massive bunker, and rolls determinedly toward the cup. That's the way designer Gary Player intended the hole to be played.

Assistant pro David Gagnon points out that there is actually another, safer way to play the hole, although it generally precludes a par: "Many players will take less club and stay short of the green in the landing area, leaving them a much easier pitch and putt than from either left or right of the green. The green is generous enough for a two-hundred yard shot, but the way it's canted left to right, you can hit the right distance and still end up in the bunker or the trees to the right or the hill on the left."

"There are a lot of strategic decisions to be made," Gagnon says. "You can get a quick double with one swing of the bat."

#15, 521 yards, par 5 - (2009) This double dogleg is a thinking man's hole, according to GlenArbor Director of Golf Rob Labritz, one of the more cerebral players in the Met PGA. There are choices to be made on almost every shot. This first choice comes on the tee: Do you favor the right side or the left side of the fairway? Too far right puts you behind trees and makes for a difficult second shot, while over-compensating to the left brings the lake into play. Assuming you avoid those problems by landing somewhere in the right half of the fairway, the second shot presents a classic risk-reward decision. Do you go for the green perched on the side of the hill and protected by a deep bunker complex or lay up to your ideal wedge distance and try to finesse a birdie? It will take some doing, since there is never an easy pin position on the wide but shallow green.

#12, 579 yards, par 5 - (2011) Director of Golf Rob Labritz, who was the low-scoring PGA club professional at last year's PGA Championship at Whistling Straits, says there are two ways to play the hole. "The long hitter can use a cut off the tee to avoid driving through the fairway and into the two bunkers that lie straight ahead," he says, "or he can use a three wood without hitting a cut." Either way, you'll still have 250 to 300 yards left to reach the green. The main thing is to stay in the fairway, since anything right or left is essentially dead—even on the second shot. Labritz recommends laying up to 100 yards, then wedging it close to the pin. Bunkers surround the green, which has a barely perceptible but highly treacherous right to left slope.

#17, 189 yards, par 3 - (2019) A perfect tee shot on the penultimate hole at GlenArbor will find the capacious green, but how many of us hit perfect tee shots? A good miss on the long par three will stay out of the bunkers (and the greenside lake) but still leave you with a tricky chip off a tight lie that you have to get close to put a par on your scorecard. Director of golf Rob Labritz says you have two options: either fly the ball to the hole with a wedge or hit a low running chip with something like an eight iron, choosing the shot where you feel the most confident.

HAMPSHIRE COUNTRY CLUB
MAMARONECK

(2016) Hampshire Country Club is back. After closing for a year before the sale to current owner New World Realty, then suffering the depredations of superstorm Sandy, the Mamaroneck club has tackled course conditioning, upgraded the clubhouse, and supercharged the staff with the hiring of Hampton Golf to manage the property. The investments have paid

off with a host of new, young families as members and kudos from the long-timers who stuck with the club through its ups and downs.

"It's been great to hear from the members about the quality of their experiences on the course," says head pro Rob Sutton. "They are very happy about course conditions, which makes play increase. Signups for programs and events has grown as a result. Guest play is up, too."

The biggest improvement has come in course conditions, which are vastly better than they've ever been, thanks to the work of course superintendent Scott Olson.

"Turf conditions have been improved steadily over the last three years," Olson says. He and his crew have done a lot of work on the drainage system, especially on the fifth and sixth holes, which are low-lying in an area with a high water table. When it rained in the past, the holes could be unplayable for quite some time. "We replaced the old clay drainage pipes with a new system that includes sump pumps," Scott says. "Now, we can monitor the lake areas and get excess water out. That gave the turf a chance to dry out." He adds that watering practices were changed too, and more drainage work is being completed this year.

"I've expanded a few of the greens back to what I believe were the original dimensions and been pretty aggressive with aerification to get the remaining salt out of them," Olson explains. Most of this past summer, greens at Hampshire were smooth and fast — about 10.5 on the Stimpmeter.

"We're leveling and realigning some of the tees to improve sight lines," Olson adds. "Next spring, we'll focus on the bunkers. They still drain and perform well, but sand depth needs to be put back to what it should be."

"Ownership is involved and committed to upgrades," points out general manager David Smith. "We have a lot of young families among the new club members and the husband, wife, and kids are all playing." New members want the family to get their money's worth, he observes. "New members are looking for programs for the whole family. So, while the father is on the course, for example, we provide junior and ladies' programs from 10 to 12." A new assistant pro, Katy Decker, has helped build the ladies' and junior golf programs.

"Afterwards, they all meet for lunch at the pool then stick around for Sunday dinner," adds director of sales Dorothy Mourousiz. "We do a barbeque on the patio overlooking the Sound. It's gorgeous." In addition to work on the golf course, the clubhouse has been completely re-carpeted and the offseason will see some work in the locker rooms.

What about the long-running legal issues stemming from the owner's development plans? "The plans have been adjusted and the scope of the development is still a work in progress," Smith points out. "It's changed from a full course closure to develop homes to keeping nine holes and town homes with some single family homes. It's yet to be determined. It's a long process. It could be years and years." In the meantime, play on the Devereux Emmet course gem continues.

HARRISON MEADOWS COUNTRY CLUB
HARRISON

Harrison Meadows #6 (JF)

(2022) Harrison Meadows is the first new daily-fee golf club to open in Westchester in nearly 15 years, although for now, at least, it will be available only to Harrison residents and their guests. The course, which has existed in one form or another on the property since 1917, was most recently Willow Ridge CC.

When the member-owned private club put itself on the market, the Town of Harrison stepped in and took it over last year and hired Troon Golf to manage it. It opened as a semiprivate club this year. Residents of the town, which includes Harrison, West Harrison, and Purchase, will be able to join as annual passholders at several levels. For now, daily-fee play will be limited to Harrison residents, as well, although that may change once the level of demand is established. This initial year for Harrison Meadows will essentially be a shakedown cruise for new ownership, new management, new staff, and new public-course golfers.

With a 71.3 course rating from the tips, Harrison Meadows is more difficult than most of the public courses in the county, but multiple tees make it playable for shorter hitters. Much of the difficulty comes from elevation climbs, like those on the ninth and eighteenth holes, both near-500-yard par fives that play straight up cardiac-arrest-inducing hills. Water is a factor on half the holes on the course.

Notable Holes

#15, 405 yards, par 4 - (2006) This is a visually appealing short par four at an often-overlooked course right next door to Westchester Country Club. The fifteenth at Willow Ridge was redesigned by Ken Dye in 2002 and now it's one of the most demanding holes on the course.

Water stretches the full length of the hole along the right before turning in front of the green to catch errant approach shots. There's a bridge to the green at the end of the fairway, which makes a handy target for those wanting to hug the left side. Namesake willow trees frame the hole on the right and a fountain accents the bucolic scene.

The hole is pretty, but the second shot is as scary as a Wes Craven movie. From anywhere you choose, it's all carry over the water. There is no bailout area to the right, although you can lay up to the left if you dare, according to club pro Tony DeMaria. "A lay-up still has water on the right and trees on the left," he points out. "After that, you're left with anywhere from 60 to 120 yards over water, and that's a scary shot."

The long, narrow green is canted away from the fairway. It's full of undulations, almost guaranteeing any putt over twelve feet will have two or more breaks. There is a tier in the back, then the green slopes severely to the front. Just to add to the danger, there is a swale in the left rear corner that feeds balls off the green.

#4, 210 yards, par 3 - (2015) Head pro John Reeves says the fourth hole has all of the elements to raise the heart rate of a scratch golfer and can be downright overwhelming for the bogey player. "It starts with the uphill 210 yards to the green that plays more like 225," he says. "The green is guarded with bunkers left, right and long, although the back bunker serves as trouble not so much on the tee shot as for second shots that are struck too thin." He points out that a miss of more than 25 yards left or right of the green means you'll be hitting three from the tee because your ball is lost or out of bounds.

Reeves adds, "Most bogey golfers want to attack a par three like they see the tour players do on TV. The best strategy for this hole is to play the tee shot short of the green. The fairway approach starts approximately 60 yards from the green, so you will have a second shot from the short grass with no bunker to carry." Take care once you're on the green, though, because the green is severely yet unnoticeably sloped from back to front. He cautions, "Putting from above the hole leads to three- or even four-putts."

HOLLOW BROOK GOLF CLUB
CORTLANDT MANOR

Hollow Brook #11 (JF)

New Owner for Hollow Brook (2010)

Hollow Brook, one of Westchester County's more interesting golf courses, changed hands recently and the new owner promises to take the facility up a notch or two while making the cost of membership more accurately reflect the realities of today's economy.

"The land is spectacular, the course wonderfully challenging and my team will be working on the little things to make Hollow Brook the greatest experience it can be for our members," says new owner Steve Torsoe. He says he plans to make the course more player friendly and adds, "We'll make Hollow Brook accessible to local residents, charities, as well as local high school and college golf teams."

The course, which opened in 2004 on 250 acres in Cortlandt Manor, was designed and built by Eric Bergstol, who also recently sold two other courses in the metropolitan area to Donald Trump. The track is noted for dramatic elevation changes and punitive rough as well as judicious use of the eponymous Hollow Brook that runs through it. It's 6,923 yards from the tips, although unless you drive it long and laser-straight, you have no business playing from the back tees.

I'll be watching to see what changes Torsoe makes to the course, which has a quirky hole or two. The eighth hole, for example, could be a good, solid 531-yard par five. It's a well-laid-out dogleg right that should reward a long drive that challenges the bunkers at the turn with a good chance to make the green in two. I say "should" because there's a huge tree on the edge of the fairway that completely blocks an aggressive second shot regardless of how well you place your drive.

Hollow Brook is very much a strategic player's golf course. There are a couple of short par fours that preclude use of a driver off the tee and more than a few approach shots where elevation changes make you think twice about club selection. Greens are large and rolling and well-bunkered. Bergstol was an early adapter of the shaggy-edge bunker, which fits well with the general ambiance of the course.

Notable Holes

#11, 420 yards, par 4 - (2021) Watch the wind and use your head when you tee it up on the number one handicap hole at Hollow Brook, says head pro Phil Eyre. "Being in the fairway off the tee is key," he says. "You can be aggressive with the driver and hold it tight to the waste area on the left to get a nice flat lie leaving you about 140 yards into the three-tier green. Or you can make a more conservative play with a three- or five-wood, laying it back to about 180 on a flat lie. If you hit between those two distances, you have an awkward hook lie with the ball above your feet, something you really don't want going into that green with water on the left. For the second shot, the ideal play is to the middle of the green, maybe a bit to the right side. It's narrow and there's a lot of trouble all around."

#5, 107 yards, par 3, - (2026) It looks so easy—maybe a half swing with a wedge—but it can be a disaster if you lose a ball by missing the green. A chasm surrounds three sides of it and the fourth side is on such a steep hillside covered with deep fescue you may need a mountain goat just to make a path to your ball. One Hollow Brook member (who asked to remain anonymous) had so many penalty strokes he couldn't remember if he scored a 24 or a 25 on the hole.

Hollow Brook #8 (JF)

#8, 550 yards, par 5 - (2016) Even at 550 yards, the eighth hole at Hollow Brook isn't the longest on the course. It has its own challenges, however, that require accuracy as well as length off the tee to make a par or better. Your first goal is to keep your drive out of the bunkers bordering the fairway. The club made the ones on the right a little more forgiving recently, but you still don't want to mess with them. Then you have to navigate over, around, or under the massive tree that stands directly in the best line for your second shot. Assuming you manage that task, a small, well-bunkered green awaits your third shot. The green has a lot of movement, too, so don't take your putts for granted.

HUDSON HILLS GOLF CLUB
OSSINING

Hudson Hills #1

(2012) The crown jewel of the six golf courses operated by Westchester County is Hudson Hills, 7,000 yards of impeccably-maintained fairways and greens woven into rugged hilltop terrain in Ossining. From the stone pillars marking the entrance to the cheerful attendant who greets you at the bag drop to the smooth and fast rolling greens, your experience at Hudson Hills resembles nothing so much as a round at one of the county's many top-notch private clubs.

The quality of play ranks up there, too. Hudson Hills stretches 6,935 yards from the tips, although the green tees at 6,323 with a 71.0 rating and 129 slope provide plenty of challenge. There are two other sets of tees to make the course enjoyable for players of all levels. The course is laid out up, down, around, and about one of the highest hills in the county, making your travels around the course an exercise in distance control through elevation management as well as shot direction. And here's a tip if in doubt about the line of your putt: it will always break away from the huge white water tower in view from just about everywhere. Something else to keep in mind on the front nine is that it wraps around the course clockwise, which means there's out of bounds and other trouble to the left on almost every hole.

Hudson Hills offers a steady diet of risk and reward, although you'll want to bring an extra sleeve of balls if you're an aggressive player because the rough can be gnarly and there are more than a few blind shots where it comes into play. The first opportunity comes on the second hole, a 502-yard par five with a semi-blind tee shot. You should aim well to the right to take advantage of the severe side slope that will push your ball to the left. A good drive to the end of the landing area will put you 230 from the green, but beware the water hazard on the right front: it's only 195 away and the fairway reverses camber to feed into it. Left is no bargain, either, since an impenetrable lateral hazard lines that side of the hole.

The five par threes range from 127 to 174 yards and elevation, as you might expect, plays a big role in club selection. Five of the nine par fours are over 400 yards. Most of them offer generous fairways, although the short fours demand high precision off the tee. The 368-yard eighth hole is particularly devilish, featuring a fescue-covered hillside on the right and a lateral hazard on the left the entire length of the fairway. Don't lay back too far from the tee, though, or you won't be able to see the green around the sharp dogleg.

HUDSON NATIONAL GOLF CLUB
CROTON

Hudson National #12 (JF)

Renovation (2023)

It happens slowly, but golf courses wear out. Just like your house needs a new roof, your golf course needs green contours restored, bunkers refreshed, and leaky irrigation systems replaced. The game itself has changed, too, so new tee boxes and bunkers and more versatile green surrounds need to be installed to accommodate both longer and shorter strikers of the golf ball. Given these needs, major renovation projects are in various stages of completion throughout the region.

One of the most extensive has begun at Hudson National Golf Club in Croton-on-Hudson, N.Y. The club will close in July to replace basically every blade of grass on the perennial top-100 golf course, re-contour the greens, update the bunkering, address some drainage issues, and replace the irrigation system. It was simply time, according to club president Phil Moyles. "We had reached an inflection point with our greens," he explains. "They were supposed to be good for 20 seasons when they were first put in, and we have stretched it out to over 25 seasons." The course opened for play in 1995.

That inflection point was really brought home at the 2021 Met Open when blistering heat toasted the greens that had been cut and rolled to major tournament green speeds. The event also exposed some needed changes to adapt the course to today's game. "I did some drive charting at the Met Open, and the guys were hitting the ball in ungodly places," says Theron Harvey, director of club operations. "We're putting new bunkers out to challenge the low-handicap player. Plus, some of our bunkers penalized the high handicapper, so we're getting rid of those. The goal is to make it more interesting." He says the club is putting more undulation in the greens, which will add challenges but also mean the superintendent doesn't have to maintain super-fast conditions all the time.

Ruins at Hudson National

Before Hudson National (2020)

Ruins from a country club that never existed compete for golfers' attention with expansive vistas of the Hudson River at the highest point on the front nine at Hudson National Golf Club. The stone chimneys, foundations, and stairs from the ill-fated Hessian Hills Country Club dominate the skyline between the third and fifth tees and the fourth green, incorporated into the routing by architect Tom Fazio. The ruins date to a pair of suspicious 1930 fires (and one in 1938) that destroyed eight of the fifteen buildings purchased from a gentleman farmer in 1926 by real estate developer Milton Gordon to serve as the campus for his doomed country club. A golf course was commissioned but never built, memberships were sold but never activated, grand openings were announced but never held. Financial shenanigans ensued and a fortuitous $100,000 insurance policy that was purchased two weeks before the fires put an end to everything except the lawsuits.

Notable Holes

#1, 486 yards, par 4 - (2006) One of the great opening holes in Westchester is the long downhill first at Hudson National. From the tee shot aimed with a little draw at the bunker on the right side of the fairway to the last putt on the complicated green, a golfer might want to use the same strategy architect Tom Fazio took when he designed the course. "It required a vast amount of dynamite and patience," he said.

The landing area is generous, over sixty yards at its widest, although it narrows to twenty-five yards near the bunker on the right. A booming 300-yard drive down the middle still leaves you 186 yards to the center of the green. Hit a hook off the tee and your ball may only be found by descendants of the Kitchawank Indians who occupied the site when Henry Hudson sailed up the river.

The green is the largest on the course, but that doesn't make it easy to hit. If you miss on the right side, you're left with an intimidating downhill chip or sand shot to a green that runs away from you and drops off into a bunker shaped like a piece from a demented jigsaw puzzle.

"It's a very, very tough starting hole," says Director of Golf Scottie Nield. "It gets you warmed up quickly."

#16, 249 yards, par 3 - (2009) The scenery beyond the hole makes it easy to lose track of your ball in flight after teeing off on this spectacular par three. The Hudson River gleams in the distance with Stony Point marking the far shore while your ball sails, hopefully, through the sky to fall on the green a long, long way down the hill. Actually, the green isn't impossible to find—it's about the size of Kansas—but it does take a solid shot to get there. Sprawling bunkers await those who under-estimate the distance to the green or (more likely) over-estimate their own prowess. If you miss the green and somehow avoid the bunkers, ball-devouring knee-high rough is your punishment, so wait until after your shot comes to earth to savor the view.

 # 18, 443 yards, par 4 - (2011) There are few holes in Westchester more spectacular than the eighteenth at Hudson National. Not only is it a gloriously difficult hole, but it presents a vista of the river that's one of the best from anywhere in the county. To get the full effect, climb up to the back tee box and take a moment to revel in the wonder of it all. But unless your name is Bubba (and your average drive is over 300 yards), don't tee off from there. You can have enough trouble making par from the regular tees. To have a chance, your drive must be in the left half of the fairway, hopefully beyond the bunker. That will leave you with a long uphill approach to a well-bunkered green.

Hudson National #5 (JF)

#5, 395 yards, par 4 - (2016) There's a lot going on around the tee at Hudson National's fifth hole. The path to the tee goes through some of the scenic ruins of the old Hessian Hills clubhouse that stood on the site a hundred years ago. They compete for your attention with the panorama of the Hudson River over the new back tee on the hole. From the regular tee box itself, you're confronted with a choice: bomb one over the trouble in the landing zone to a narrow strip of fairway and a steeply downhill lie or play it safe with a 200-yard shot to a level lie and a mid- to short-iron in.

KNOLLWOOD COUNTRY CLUB
ELMSFORD

Knollwood #18

Centennial Celebration (2019)

Believed to be the oldest eighteen-hole private golf course at the same location in the country, Knollwood Country Club celebrates its 125th anniversary this year. The history of the Elmsford club is studded with notables from America's golden age of golf and commerce like John Archbold, of Standard Oil, the first president of Knollwood Country Club when it was organized in 1894.

One of the original members, civil engineer Lawrence Van Etten, laid out the first course, an eighteen-hole par 69 track. The club acquired some additional land on the recommendation of A.W. Tillinghast and hired Seth Raynor to design a new course. Raynor died before the project was completed, however, and Charles "Steamshovel" Banks finished it in 1927.

Knollwood was nationally-known in the early days of the game. Luminaries like Francis Ouimet, winner of the milestone 1913 US Open, played at Knollwood as did Bobby Jones. A plaque in the grillroom commemorates the oft-repeated legend that Jones met with Knollwood member Clifford Roberts there to plan the creation of Augusta National.

But Knollwood hasn't rested on its history. A $1.5 million restoration of the golf course was completed last year. Most of the bunkers on the course were rebuilt to match Raynor's original design, many superfluous trees were removed, some fairways re-routed, new tee boxes built, and several greens were recontoured. Today, the Knollwood amenities include tennis courts, bocce courts, a swimming pool, and several drink and dining venues.

New Ownership (2021)

Knollwood Country Club, founded in Elmsford in 1894, is now under the management of Heritage Golf Group, a boutique golf management company that acquired the club from the members under a long-term lease with an option to buy. Heritage CEO Mark Burnett says the company plans a minimum of $4 million in capital improvements to the club.

"We will immediately start with improvements to the golf course," Burnett says. Tee boxes will be refreshed, trees removed, drainage problems addressed, and cart paths are being resurfaced. "We don't anticipate changes to the way the course plays, though," Burnett says. "We really like the classic layout. It's what this place is all about." Knollwood completed a major redo of the course five years ago that restored many of the details of the Seth Raynor and Charles Banks design that had been lost over time, so Heritage's goal is to clean up some things that weren't done then.

The amenities and facilities will get major overhauls in phases, according to Burnett, beginning with the private events side of the clubhouse and the locker rooms, which will be rejuvenated with new carpet, paint, and lighting. Next to come will be an extensive remodeling of the main clubhouse building with a new dining room, revamped grill room, and addition of a large outdoor seating area with firepits and large-screen TVs. The tennis area will be fixed up and pickle ball may be added. Cabanas will be built in the pool area along with other enhancements. Still to be decided is what will be done with the building that currently houses the pro shop, carts, and some pool amenities. Ideas being floated include a fitness center and studios for golf simulators, yoga, and other club activities.

Notable Holes

#18, 432 yards, par 4 - (2006) If you can fade your tee shot on this hole, a double dogleg, you'll set up a workable approach to the fortress-like green. Slice it and you're in the drink and hook it and you've left yourself a mountain to climb.

According to club pro Bob Miller, Jr., the hole is deceiving from the tee; there's more room on the right than you think. "If you pull the ball a little bit, though, you've got no shot to get over the water," he says. It also plays a little shorter than the measured distance since the tee is elevated.

The second shot over the creek is the real test. Knollwood member Bill Losapio says, "It gives you a chance to make a par but it penalizes you if you miss a shot. You really have to be on target with your second shot." The shot to the green must avoid a bunker on the hillside left and a steep drop-off to the creek that runs past.

#13, 379 yards, par 4 – (2008) There are two successive risk and reward holes at Knollwood and we had a tough time choosing between them. The thirteenth won, mainly because the risk is one a sane person might actually take and have a chance to pull off. All it takes is a high drive over the trees that form the 90-degree right dogleg. Head Pro Bob Miller advises, "It plays shorter than the measured distance because it's downhill. Aim it just left of the tenth green. If you carry it far enough, you can hit the thirteenth green." Miss in any one of several directions, though, and you'll need at best a delicate sand wedge or at worst a chainsaw to get to the green for something north of par. After the thirteenth hole, you get to play another risk and reward hole, a short par four that's perfectly drive-able if you carry a howitzer in your bag that can blast the ball 287 yards horizontally and 50 yards vertically over the pines to drop straight down onto a green the size of a bottle cap.

LAKE ISLE COUNTRY CLUB
EASTCHESTER

Lake Isle's Devereux Emmet course epitomizes classic shotmaker's golf. The short-but-challenging course presents the full spectrum of short and long holes, as well as straight and crooked, uphill and downhill. You'll play over or around water, navigate blind shots, and use every club in your bag — perhaps even off the tee! The course opens with a pair of short par 4s and a par 3, then smacks you in the face with a trio of the toughest holes in town: the 425-yard, par 4 fourth; 400-yard, uphill-dogleg fifth; and the 449-yard, par 4 sixth. After you catch your breath, you get to tackle the 230-yard, par 3 ninth hole to finish the opening nine.

The back side has several captivating and challenging holes, including the 396-yard, downhill, severe-dogleg sixteenth, with water in play off the tee, and the 280-yard, precision-required eighteenth, one of the most fun holes in Westchester.

LEEWOOD COUNTRY CLUB
EASTCHESTER

Leewood #15 (JF)

Centennial Celebration (2022)

Leewood GC in Eastchester celebrates its rich 100-year history this year with a series of events that illustrate its place in the lives of its members, staff, and neighbors. "We've built our celebration around a concept of three Cs," says Leewood VP Greg Messerle. "They are Community, Celebration, and Carrying Forward."

Highlighting the club's dedication to its community is a special campaign to raise $100,000 for six local organizations, including the First Tee, Boys and Girls Club, and the Westchester Diaper Bank. As part of the fundraising campaign, the club will sell pavers to be installed in a centennial plaza that will also feature a 100-year time capsule to be filled by children from the many families that belong to Leewood.

Leewood was founded in 1922 by a group of local residents, including motion-picture director D.W. Griffith. The charter members purchased a certificate for $250 and paid annual dues of $50. They financed the construction of a clubhouse that opened two years later and was designed by Henry Bacon, the architect of the Lincoln Memorial.

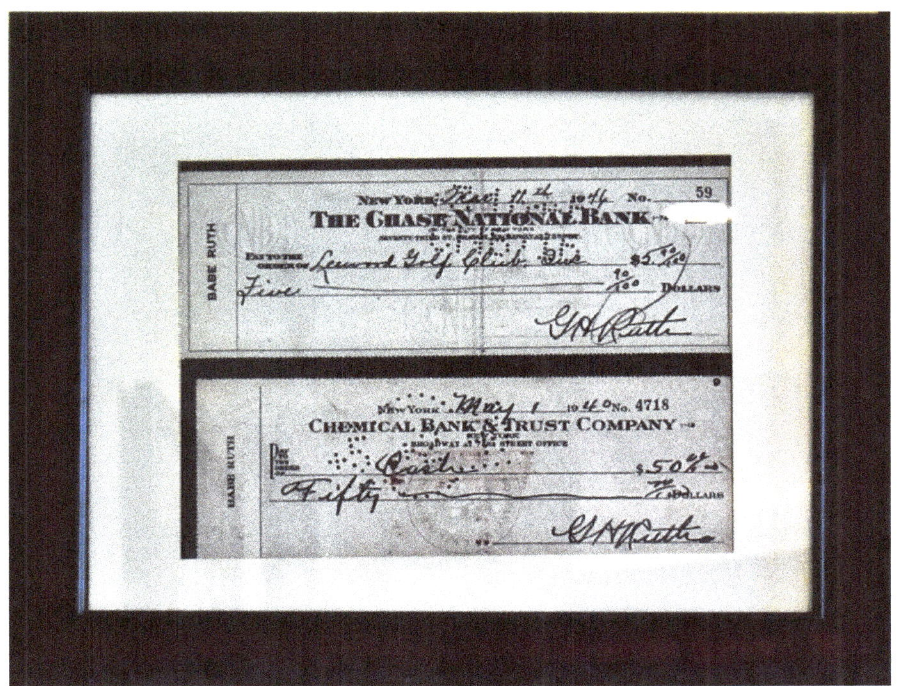

Babe Ruth Memorabilia at Leewood

The most famous member of Leewood is undoubtedly New York Yankee slugger Babe Ruth. A room in the clubhouse celebrates the Babe's membership, and the club annually holds "The Bambino," an invitational tournament that draws top players from throughout the metro region. The Babe donated two of his Leewood golf trophies for display in the Baseball Hall of Fame.

Leewood's golf course was designed by Devereux Emmet and is known for tight fairways and wicked greens, making it a classic Westchester course. The club has kept the course up-to-date with the modern game, however, with significant renovations over the last decade that included additional length for longer hitters and placement of forward tees to accommodate other players. While Leewood is celebrating its past, it has an eye on the future, according to Messerle, expanding its water-retention ponds to capture more rainwater and runoff, restricting chemical application, and utilizing natural grasses in many areas off the fairways.

Notable Holes

#18, 408 yards, par 4 - (2013) "Eighteen has gone through a major transformation," says head pro Dean Johnson. "It may now be one of the strongest holes on the course. In all my years playing in the Met Section, it's definitely now one of the best finishing holes I've played. You have a shot coming into the green that has a creek down the right, and the green feeds down to the water. We put a trap left. If you aim right you're pointed at trouble, and if you pull your shot left you're going right at the bunker. We have tall fescue behind the green, so a little bit long and you're in trouble there.

"It's very hard but very fair. For the average player who hits a drive 210 yards, you'll have 180 yards in there. There's ample landing area in front of the green, and it's a little bit bigger than most of the greens here at Leewood—but it's your finishing hole, so you don't want to end with anything worse than a par. That will put some butterflies in your gut."

#11, 136 yards, par 3 - (2016) If you don't love the eleventh hole at Leewood, you don't have a soul. Take a moment to enjoy the view from the tee high above the green. Admire the picture-perfect stone-wall-bordered pond you'll have to carry when you swing away. Let your eye wander to the line of colorful ornamental trees behind the green, then note that they're also behind two of the three bunkers surrounding it—bunkers you don't want to blast out of too often since the green slopes steeply from back to front. The eleventh hole got a new tee box during the recent renovation at Leewood, one that just adds to the simple pleasures of this pleasing short par three.

#17 par 4, 307 yards - (2026) The original tee box—the one played by Babe Ruth when he was a member—has been restored on this hole, which revives the legend that the Sultan of Swat often leveraged his homerun power to drive the green. Of course, the trees that line the right side of the fairway were not nearly as tall as they are today. Then there is the pond we lay up to now. In the Babe's day it was no more than a narrow creek.

LINKS AT VALLEY FIELDS
YORKTOWN

Links at Valley Fields #9

(2024) A long-delayed dream came true last year when The Links at Valley Fields finally opened for play in Yorktown. The par three nine-hole course, operated by Yorktown Golf Group on parkland owned by the town, is a fully-functioning golf facility with pro shop, lessons, golf carts for those with mobility issues, and a restaurant, the Tee Bar & Grille, that's proven to be quite an attraction in its own right.

The well-conditioned course, which was built on the site of an abandoned nine-hole course in Shrub Oak, has three sets of tees for holes ranging from 96 to 202 yards in length. It's the perfect place for experienced players to hone their short game or youngsters to pick up the sport.

MAPLE MOOR GOLF CLUB
WHITE PLAINS

(2010) Maple Moor is the county's most-played course, logging some 52,000 rounds annually. The course's popularity is partly explained by its location just off the Hutchinson River parkway in White Plains and partly by the player-friendly nature of the course. Aside from the abundance of maple trees lining several fairways and water in play on six holes, most of Maple Moor's holes are straightforward and perfectly par-able, although you'll need to check your club selection on several of the steeply-uphill approach shots.

The ninth hole presents two of the most difficult challenges on the course. At 434 yards, it requires a long approach shot to an elevated green. Miss left and your ball will tumble downhill to oblivion. Miss right and you're chipping downhill and hoping your ball won't scoot across the green to the afore-mentioned disaster area. The second challenge comes after you've finished the hole and have to climb heart-attack hill, aka the path to the tenth tee.

(2021) Golfers at Maple Moor come off the course drier and happier now that the county has finished its multimillion-dollar drainage-and-irrigation project. Course conditions are the best they've ever been thanks to the creation of three retention ponds along the eighth fairway and elevation of portions of the ninth fairway by a full five feet above the previous waterlogged level. The improvements helped playing conditions but didn't change the character of the short-but-tight course, which typically receives more play than any of the other five. The sixth hole, for example, is still a tough par five even though it's only 470 yards long. A drive anywhere right of center on the fairway will block the second shot approach and force a lay-up to the elevated green.

METROPOLIS COUNTRY CLUB
WHITE PLAINS

Metropolis #6 (JF)

Building on its Past (2022)

Fresh off the celebration of its centennial, Metropolis Country Club figures it has the formula for member satisfaction. "At the end of the day," says club president Harold Grunfeld, "if you give people a great golf course, good service, and real good food, it makes them very happy."

Metropolis had been successfully making members happy for a long time, and when Covid hit, says Grunfeld, the unfortunate situation opened many new eyes to how well it does it: "Members played more and brought more guests to play, so we got more exposure for the golf course. That, coupled with the dinners and lunches they enjoyed on the terrace, created even more interest in the club."

Metropolis Country Club was incorporated in 1922 by 18 members of the Metropolis City Club, a social and dining organization located on Fifty-Seventh Street in Manhattan and founded in 1879 "to promote social intercourse among its members and to encourage musical, literary, dramatic and other recreative exercises and to establish a library." The members acquired an eighteen-hole course built by Herbert Strong in 1904 for Century Country Club, which in turn moved to its present site in nearby Purchase.

The new owners upgraded the locker room and other amenities to the existing white-columned clubhouse and added a swimming pool, beginning its evolution into a family club. They also purchased more land and, in 1929, hired A.W. Tillinghast to redesign the course. Tilly is credited with the current seventh, twelfth, thirteenth, and fourteenth holes. In the early 1970's, the club converted a portion of the course into badly-needed parking, and architect Joe Finger designed the new fifteenth and sixteenth holes that replaced the previous ones. Finger's partner, Ken Dye, came in 1998 to revamp the course.

The course today
Today's course bears the influence of Ron Forse, who was hired in 2013 to oversee a total renovation that was completed in 2015. "When he came in, we tried to put the golf course back to its original intent, not restore the exact original layout," explains course superintendent David McCaffery. "We had about 60 bunkers when we started and they all got rebuilt and redesigned. We tried to make it play fair for everyone. All the approaches had been pinched, allowing for no run-up shots. We changed that and expanded all the greens back to original size. We added most of the fairway bunkers back in, did a lot of tree removal, and took out flower boxes and planting beds to get a more natural look. We also added areas of native fescue to add definition."

The result is a 6,827-yard par 70 layout from the tips that members play at par 71 for 6,587 yards. The property features a ridge on the center line that falls away in both directions. Head pro Craig Thomas says, "There are few level lies in the fairway. There are holes that go right to left and some that go the other way. You really have to think your way around the course."

Metropolis has hosted every major Met Area professional and amateur championship, including three Met Amateurs, one Ike, two Met Senior Opens, and four Met Opens. Among the winners of note, Jackie Burke, Jr., the home pro, won the 1949 Met Open by six shots over Gene Sarazen in the renewal of the championship after an eight-year hiatus. Metropolis was the site where Dick Siderowf won the first of his five Met Amateur Championships in 1968 and his fifth 21 years later in 1989.

Pro shop notables

Metropolis has long had a stellar reputation for the play of its golf pros, three of whom were inducted into the World Golf Hall of Fame. Paul Runyan, aka "Little Poison," won the 1934 and 1938 PGA Championships and many other national events while representing the club. Jackie Burke, Jr., was the pro for several years after World War II until he joined the PGA Tour full-time; he went on to win the Masters and the PGA Championship in 1956. "Lighthorse" Harry Cooper, who amassed 30 victories on the PGA Tour—the most by anyone who never won one of the four majors— was head pro at the club from 1953 to 1978.

Metropolis head pro Craig Thomas on the lesson tee (JF)

In more recent times, Yonkers native Gene Borek, head pro from 1980 to 2005, won three Met PGA Championships and took part in eleven PGA Championships and ten US Opens. Borek, who got into the field for the 1973 Open at Oakmont as an alternate just two days before it started, drew national attention when he shot a course-record 65 in the second round, a mark broken just two days later by Johnny Miller's 63. Borek's successor, Ron Philo, won the PGA Professional National Championship and the Met PGA in 2006 while he was head pro at the club. Current head pro Craig Thomas, who came to Metropolis in 2007, has competed in four PGA Championships, four PGA Seniors, and the US Senior Open. He won the MGA Senior Open in 2013. Thomas held the course record at Bethpage

Black (64) until it was broken by Brooks Koepka at the 2019 PGA Championship.

These accomplished players weren't hired by accident, according to club VP Andy Nathan. "It's been part of the culture of the club for a hundred years," he says. "That caliber of player tends to attract other good assistant pros and even interns to the club, so we've always had a great teaching staff. Plus, it brings us a non-local perspective on the operation because they see other very good venues as they compete around the country."

Course conditions count

Great players are drawn to great courses, and Metropolis keeps its 18 holes in top condition. Looking forward, the club has recently deepened its retention ponds, dug four wells, and installed a new pump station in a big step to become self-sufficient with water. "The way the weather is changing, we didn't want to get to the point where the city says we can't buy any water," McCaffrey says. Next year, they will replace the 1989-vintage irrigation system with a new two-wire system that provides feedback and lets the staff control every sprinkler head individually.

Also next year, Metropolis will close on the sale of five acres of land where the club's current entrance and maintenance buildings are located along Dobbs Ferry Road, to Brightview Senior Living. A new and much more attractive entrance will be built, and maintenance operations will move to a spot in a different corner of the course. "We didn't have other uses for the new maintenance corner," Nathan says. "It doesn't affect the course one iota." The Brightview building will be built into the hillside at street level, so it will basically be out of sight from the club.

The sale and its proceeds are just one more way Metropolis is enhancing its prospects for the future. This spring, it opened an upgraded aquatic center with a completely new pool, a new kiddie pool, new decking, a renovated pool house and locker rooms, and fresh landscaping. It also built a new game room and playground for the kids. There's now an outdoor sitting area that transitions from the golf range to the pool so members and their guests can relax in Adirondack chairs and watch the activity around them. The club also created an additional "nineteenth hole" nearby where parents can eat and drink while keeping an eye on the pool.

In 2019, Metropolis stepped up its culinary game, too, by hiring executive chef Chris Gesualdi. Chef Chris has a resume to match that of the club's golf professionals: He was right-hand to legendary chef Thomas Keller at La Reserve, executive chef of Montrachet, and a teacher at the Institute of Culinary Education in Manhattan for ten years. His arrival enabled the club to provide exceptional food everywhere from the pool house to the main dining room to the 300-seat terrace overlooking the golf course.

Metropolis has put itself in position for continual long-term growth by actively working to draw new members based on the quality of the experience, not the price of the membership. To keep that going, the club needs to appeal to every member of the family—and it's doing just that.

"We've seen a significant trend of younger members from various groups," Grunfeld says. "We have a group of new single-digit young golfers who haven't started families yet. But we also have more and more young families joining, which bodes great for the future. Our tennis program has grown more robust over the years, and as tennis or social members spend time at the club, they become golf members as well. It's a positive trend with new blood coming in."

As Thomas puts it, "The club's in a good place right now. Every club has challenges, but everything seems to be aligned here now. Food's good, golf's good, what more do you need?"

Notable Holes

#6, 423 yards, par 4 - (2006) Now we take a trip to Augusta National—or is it Metropolis? That's what popular tour pro Peter Jacobsen said when he stood on the tee looking through the cathedral of trees to where the fairway disappears downhill to the left on this sweeping dogleg.

The fairway falls off dramatically from the tee. There is a huge bunker on the right corner about 240 yards away, although it's partially hidden by two spectacular dogwoods. The green poses Augusta-like against a gorgeous backdrop of azaleas and rhododendrons whose color is replaced by annual flower beds in the summer. There is a picturesque pond to the right, although it's not really in play.

Metropolis head pro Gene Borek, who retired last year after 25 years at the club, says, "It's a hole that will keep you busy."

The approach is full of deception. It appears to be downhill, but the elevated green eliminates that advantage. There is a trap in front of the green that looks very small from the fairway, mainly because the green is so wide, but the bunker is fourteen yards long and only about four yards from the front, so it can cause plenty of trouble. Running through the shallow green leaves you with an impossible chip back down the narrow, severely-canted green.

It's a beautiful hole that can rip your heart out on the second shot.

#7, 438 yards, par 4 - (2009) So much has been written about the sixth hole at Metropolis that the deceptively challenging par four that follows it is frequently overlooked. The visual tricks begin on the tee, where you're facing what appears to be a wide open fairway, plagued only slightly by a bunker to the right and a heavily wooded hillside that couldn't possibly come into play—or could it? And that creek on the left isn't really in play either, is it? Assuming your drive is on the right half of the fairway (anything left will feed into the rough where trees will block the approach) and stays out of that pesky bunker, you'll have an uphill approach over another bunker that appears to be greenside, but actually has a 35-yard landing area behind it. Just be sure to land your ball on the right side of the green, since everything moves hard left once it starts rolling.

#12, 457 yards, par 4 - (2010) The shape of the land serves as a guide to the shape of your shot on this risk-and-reward dogleg. The perfect drive is a long draw to the left center of the fairway, which will catch the hill and leave you a mid- or short-iron approach from a level lie. Don't feel up to hitting a 270-yard draw? Aim for the center of the fairway and plan on a long second shot from the top of the hill. The hole plays downhill, though, so you can probably hit a club or so less than the measured distance, and the bunkers on the left aren't particularly obnoxious. The green is one of the flattest putting surfaces on the course, so getting on in regulation can bring you a par or better if you don't read more break into the putt than really exists.

MOHANSIC GOLF CLUB
CORTLANDT MANOR

Mohansic #4

(2010) Westchester County-owned golf got its start in 1925 when Mohansic Golf Course opened in Yorktown. The course has long been considered the most difficult of the five original county courses, with a combination of moderate length, tight fairways, and small, fast greens.

Two of the more challenging holes come early in your round. The third is a 425-yard par four that begins with a blind tee shot to a narrow, tree-lined fairway. You may also want to hit a longer-than-expected club for your approach, too, since the green is uphill. Once you're on the putting surface, take a few extra moments to line up your shot—the green is more treacherous than it looks. The fourth hole, a 442 yard par four, calls for a draw around the corner on the uphill dogleg. If your normal tee shot is a fade, aim for the white pine on the corner and hope. It's a tough tee shot since the fairway slopes left to right. Your approach on the fourth hole is to an elevated green protected by bunkers on both sides.

MOUNT KISCO COUNTRY CLUB
MOUNT KISCO

Mount Kisco #10 (JF)

Major Renovation (2022)

Mount Kisco Country Club recently announced the start of a major renovation under the guidance of architect Stephen Kay. This summer, the 92-year-old club began work on restoration of its bunkers and several tee boxes as well as selective tree removal to improve turf conditions.

Kay explained that the bunkers had been redone in the 1990s in a project that changed them from having flash faces to grass faces. Over the years, many of the grass sides had encroached on the sand bottoms to create narrow bunkers that were nearly impossible to play. The original 1930 design by Tom Winton featured flash faces as revealed by pre-WWII aerial photos Kay referenced in creating the new bunkers. As part of the project, many fairway bunkers will also be moved to reflect the modern game.

Club President Vinny Nagler says, "The membership decided it's time for us to bring the golf course up to a new level." He added that a new pool deck and tennis bubble are in the works as well.

The "bones" of the course won't be changed, according to Nagler. Its flavor as a parkland layout has proven popular with players at all levels and has withstood the test of time. A natural system of streams crosses thirteen of the holes, creating both natural hazards and picturesque scenes for golfers on the course.

Multi-purpose Barn/Playhouse (2020)

Henry Fonda was a golfer, but in the 1930s he was perhaps better known locally for treading the boards at the Westchester Playhouse, a summer stock theater that was a feature of the Lawrence Farms Community, the predecessor of Mount Kisco CC. The playhouse still stands today, well preserved and in use as the principle maintenance facility for the club. The building's original function, a barn to house prized livestock, is reflected in the weather vanes atop the twin cupolas on the roof.

Notable Holes

#5, 453 yards, par 4 - (2012) You don't normally expect an impossible green on a long par four, but that's what sits at the top of the hill on Mount Kisco's fifth hole. The green doesn't just slope from the back left to front right—it falls away like the deck of the Titanic just before it slipped beneath the waves. In other words, don't try to putt from above the hole.

First you have to get there, of course, and that's a long, uphill battle. Literally. The fairway slopes from left to right, so slicers and faders are at a distinct disadvantage. Even a good drive to the left center will leave you with an uphill, side-hill lie for your second shot, which will probably be with a fairway wood since the USGA prohibits the use of rocket launchers. Many members play this conservatively as a par five. Considering the many ways a four can turn into a seven on this hole, that's not a bad idea.

(2018) The "new" fifth hole at Mount Kisco isn't necessarily any easier (how do you make a 453-yard uphill par four "easy"!?) but its green is a lot more reasonable following the recent recontouring of its punitive false front and back tier.

OLD OAKS COUNTRY CLUB
PURCHASE

Old Oaks #18 and clubhouse (JF)

Deep Roots (2019)

With a golf course created by two legendary Golden Age architects and a spectacular mansion for a clubhouse, Old Oaks Country Club could easily sit on its considerable laurels and bask in the glories of days gone by. But the 94-year-old Purchase, N.Y., club is focused on the future instead.

"We're trying to provide what young families want," says President Josh Polan, "We've tried to broaden the mix of our membership, too." Like so many private clubs, Old Oaks lost some members in the aftermath of the 2008 national economic meltdown. It fought back aggressively, though, and today has a robust membership of 400 families. Roughly 50 of them have been members for two or even three generations while an equal number are new within the last ten years.

"When things got tough, the board recognized the situation and went after some new members," according to head golf professional Nick Maselli. "They also placed a big bet on golf. The club spent $3.5 million on the golf course, the range, and the short game area, and it's paid off. People are coming and they're excited about it."

Old Oaks has purposefully stepped up its amenities and significantly modernized its attitude. "We've tried to reduce the formality of the club," Polan says. "There was a time when, on Saturday nights, men wore jackets and ties. My guess is now there are maybe three nights a year when jackets are requested and ties aren't required at all.

"We've taken in a lot of members and the churn has been remarkably small. That tells me we're accomplishing what we set out to do. A number of these people joined when our initiation fee was peanuts. They could have left after a year or two without losing much, but they haven't."

From the city to the country

Members of the Progress City Club, a group of businessmen in Manhattan, organized what eventually became Old Oaks Country Club in 1925 to expand the club's activities beyond swimming, billiards, and card-playing in its home at Central Park West and 87th Street. It began as the Progress Country Club on the current site, then was renamed Purchase Country Club, Pine Ridge Country Club, and finally became Old Oaks Country Club when it merged with Tuckahoe's Oak Ridge Country Club during the Great Depression.

Legend has it that the "Old Oaks" name was derived not from the trees on the course but from the logos on the Oak Ridge CC dinnerware that was put into use as a money-saving measure after the merger. Today, the most prominent display of oak trees at the club is the allée that leads from the impressive stone pillars at the entrance. The red oaks were planted in 1988 to replace double rows of Norway maples that originally lined the road.

The Progress City Club acquired the 205-acre estate of William Read (of investment bank Dillon Read, & Co. fame) from his widow for $600,000 and immediately put A.W. Tillinghast to work designing two golf courses. The nine-hole West Course opened in 1926, and members began play on the eighteen-hole East Course the next year. The courses were actually constructed by Charles Alison of Alison and Holt using Tillinghast's designs. Tilly had resigned when the cost of construction exceeded the $100,000 specified in his contract, which carried a clause that reduced his fee if he exceeded the budget. Alison was already also building Century Country Club, which abutted Old Oaks before the bulk of the West Course was obliterated by the construction of I-684 in 1963.

Reimagining the course

Like most Golden Age golf courses, Old Oaks has undergone many changes, although the routing and the muscular character of the track remain the same. It's formidable enough to co-host sectional qualifying for the US Open along with Century CC on a three-year rotation with Canoe Brook CC since 1987. Old Oaks will also host the Met PGA Championship in 2021 and the Met Amateur in 2025, the club's centennial year.

Third-generation member, club historian, and former president Ken Schlechter says, "It was a real turning point when Lowell Schulman became president. He made a lot of improvements in the course and hired a professional greens superintendent. The quality was really stepped up." Schulman's long association with the club is memorialized by a plaque near the lake on the sixth hole proclaiming it "Loch Lowell."

In 2001, Ken Dye toughened the course by lengthening it, deepening the bunkers, and constructing a new eighteenth green. In 2016, Rees Jones began phase one of a master plan that called for undoing some of those modern touches and restoring its classical character, including replacement of that eighteenth green. "It had five tiers!" exclaims Maselli. "The new one is much more traditional in a Tillinghast sort of way. It's back-to-front with subtle breaks. The green is now kidney-shaped and has a bunker right front that matches the rest of the golf course."

The Rees Jones renovations were designed not to make the course more difficult—with a 71.9/140 Course and Slope Rating from the 6,421-yard blue tees, it's already tough enough for most mortal golfers—but to provide more flexibility. New tee boxes were created on half the holes. "It was a combination of black, a couple of blues, and many red and green tees," Maselli explains. "We wanted to spread the golf course out more so every skill level had a course to play."

A big part of the master plan was a major upgrade to the club's practice facilities. A double-ended range is complemented by a short game complex with two target greens, three bunkers, and countless lie/turf variations. All the bunkers can be played in both directions so you can work on short as well as long sand recoveries. And Maselli notes a well-appreciated detail: "We put good balls there so if you're chipping, you're not hitting a hard range ball."

Another enhancement intended to attract more family use of the golf course is a state-of-the-art indoor practice facility. "It has three hitting bays, a putting green, and a lounge," Maselli says. "All the bays are equipped with advanced technology. The teaching bay has Flight Scope and V-1 cameras. The other two have Foresight with desktop Dell gaming computers with big monitors so members can use them without taking a lesson."

The investment has paid off, as the bays were in steady use throughout the normally slow winter months. "It's been a big attraction with all the new members that are local families," Maselli says. "Saturday is their family day together and coming to the indoor golf facility becomes just like going to basketball practice or whatever. Without the technology, kids wouldn't be interested."

Maselli, who has been head pro since 2017, started at the club eighteen years ago as an assistant to Bobby Heins, whose playing credentials include back-to-back Met Open triumphs as well as nearly every other title in the area, not to mention competing in 15 major championships. The original Progress City Club head pro was "Wild Bill" Melhorn, who lasted just a year before he moved to Fenway GC and was replaced by Bobby Cruickshank, perhaps best remembered for losing to 21-year-old Bobby Jones in a playoff at the 1921 US Open at Inwood. Willie MacFarland, who beat Jones in the 1925 US Open, became head pro in 1936 when the club merged with Oak Ridge and became today's Old Oaks.

Old Oaks #8 (JF)

A dramatic clubhouse

The golf facilities are excellent, but it's the clubhouse at Old Oaks that takes the experience to a dramatic and literal peak. The English-style manor house was constructed in 1890 as a "summer cottage" by Trenor Luther Park, a Manhattan merchant and commodore of the New York Yacht Club.

To enhance his summer home, Park hired Beatrix Jones Farrand, who designed the White House's Rose Garden, to landscape the grounds.

Park sold the estate, known as "Hill Crest," to William Read in 1906, and Read added more property to the grounds as well as rooms to the already-sumptuous mansion to make space for his nine children. "We've had renovations, but basically the character has stayed the same," Schlechter says. "I love the Grand Hall. The craftsmanship is wonderful." Iwona Sterk, the general manager since 2017, explains that the club takes great care to restore furnishings to match the original fabrics and finishes because the members appreciate the artistry. Today, the 80,000-square-foot clubhouse has some fifty rooms including three indoor dining facilities, outdoor cocktail and dining terraces, locker rooms, an exercise room, and apartments for members.

Just as the golf course and practice facility have been transformed to attract a wider array of family members, other club amenities have been modernized with the same goal in mind. "Our membership is very diverse," Sterk says. "We have legacies in their nineties and families with young children. It can be a challenge pleasing everyone, but we make sure there are activities for all on our calendar."

Among those family-friendly innovations is the Old Oaks Treehouse, a space where kids can hang out while their parents enjoy other parts of the club. "The room not only has games and other activities, but we hire two teachers for the season," Sterk explains. "We also have a playground and basketball court, and the teachers take the kids to tennis, golf, and swimming lessons."

The Olympic-size pool and adjacent kiddie pool, both classically landscaped, are centerpieces of club life at Old Oaks as well as the site of some semi-historic occurrences. "Having Ali McGraw swim topless in our swimming pool during the filming of *Goodbye, Columbus* was quite a significant event," says Schlechter.

Old Oaks offers a wide variety of dining options, from the classically impressive Oak Room to the chicly modern Acorn Grill, not to mention the unique halfway house, where Efrain Barajas has presided since 1987. The lakeside facility not only serves golfers from its site at the confluence of seven greens and tees, but is a favorite for member families who enjoy casual dinners there on Wednesday and Saturday evenings that are typically sold out throughout the season.

Another unique food feature at Old Oaks is Acorn Organics Farm, which occupies five acres where the original estate gardens were located. The brainchild of former Old Oaks president Richard Fleder and member Andrew Benerofe, the farm not only provides spectacularly fresh produce for the ever-changing menus at Old Oaks, but the club donates about

60,000 pounds of food annually to local pantries and other organizations through the Old Oaks Foundation. Members can also pay into a crop-share program for their own tables.

Old Oaks Country Club celebrates its past while it lays the groundwork for its future in a coterie of loyal members. "New members are surprised at how easy it is to integrate themselves into the membership," Polan points out. "Some clubs are tough. If you don't know a lot of people it can be very hard. We do a solid job of making sure new members get comfortable, not only with the facilities, but with the other members as quickly as possible. If they don't, they're not going to be happy. Golf is a social activity and we do a pretty good job of getting people to know each other and feel comfortable."

Sterk adds, "This is all done to build the next generation of members."

That next generation of members is perfectly exemplified by the Herzig siblings, Gabby and Robbie, who won the club's championships last year. Gabby, who was a 19-year-old sophomore at Pomona College, won the women's title in her first try while 15-year-old Robbie beat a five-time club champion in a playoff to capture the men's title. It was his first attempt as well. As Polan says, "That's what we mean when we talk about young members and the ability to grow young players."

Notable Holes

#18, 547 yards, par 5 - (2006) Pump up your muscles for three long shots up the hill at Old Oaks's eighteenth. Don't worry about getting there in two; if you are merely human, you simply can't.

The view from the tee is one of wide open spaces, but it doesn't include a flagstick or even a green. You can just barely make out the huge bunker that fronts the green way far away in the distance. You also see two very imposing bunkers on the right at the gentle dogleg. Just to add to the fun, head pro Bobby Heins adds, "Your drive always seems to be into the prevailing wind out of the west or with a north wind pushing you out of bounds."

"For your second shot, you have a lot of options depending on how long you are," says club pro Nick Maselli. "You can lay it up to the 150 marker, which is short of the fairway bunkers. Or you can hit a fairway wood or long iron and fly it over the bunkers, leaving yourself a wedge shot in. If you're anywhere from the 250 to the 150 marker, it's a sidehill, uphill lie."

"If and when you finally get to the green, the fun is just beginning," Heins says. When Ken Dye redesigned the hole a couple of years ago, the green was elevated seven feet above the fairway. To the right is the deepest bunker on the course and maybe in all of Westchester county, which runs nearly the full length of the 37-yard-long green. Once you finally have the flat stick in your hand, a two-putt is anything but assured because, as Heins explains, "You've got three levels on the green and it's very sloping."

#9, 378 yards, par 4 - (2007) The ninth hole at Old Oaks is best played backwards. If you're smart, you'll figure out how long you want your second shot to be, then play accordingly off the tee. Why? Because the pond that stretches across the entire approach to the green practically laps at the putting surface, so you're either wet or you're putting after your approach.

The water isn't in play from the tee and the fairway is generous, so a driver is tempting. If you pull it left, you can reach the creek in the rough, but a big drive with a little fade on it would be perfect. The problem is, that will leave you with the dreaded half wedge, a shot dependent for success on distance control—exactly what you don't want to deal with when you're trying to pitch over a watery golf ball graveyard.

Head Pro Bobby Heins says, "A smart play is a three wood or a hybrid off the tee. That sets you up for a full wedge or short iron."

#17, 425 yards, par 4 - (2009) An altimeter rather than a tape measure might be the best way to measure the true distance on this tough dogleg left. The tee shot is uphill—and needs to draw to stay in the fairway—and the second shot is even more uphill. Even if you reach the green in regulation, danger awaits if the hole is cut anywhere close to the false front. More than one aggressive putter has watched his or her ball roll back down the hill so that the climb begins all over again.

#6, 368 yards, par 4 - (2026) What appears to be a fairly benign par four becomes a tortuous memory to players with an overcooked draw. So it was with longtime member and club president Lowell Schulman, whose tee shot was sucked into the pond that lines the left of the fairway so many times that it was named "Loch Lowell" in his good-humored honor.

PEHQUENAKONCK COUNTRY CLUB
NORTH SALEM

Winged Foot wasn't the only Westchester club celebrating its 100th birthday in 2023. North Salem's Pehquenakonck Country Club opened in 1923 as well. The "Peke" as it is known, is an under-appreciated nine-hole gem of a course that features 2,012 yards of shot-makers golf with mind-bending doglegs and heart-thumping elevation changes.

The tree-lined fairways are routed through hilly, rocky terrain like that around the fourth hole, a straight uphill 115-yard par 3 justifiably known as "Mt. Kilimanjaro." The club is semi-private and is known for welcoming youngsters and others new to the game.

PELHAM COUNTRY CLUB
PELHAM

Pelham #4 (JF)

Big Changes for the Ages (2021)

It's a short but rugged climb to the top of Mount Tom in the center of Pelham Country Club's golf course, but the view is worth it. You won't see the Manhattan skyline, but you can see six radically remodeled holes that are winning national recognition for the venerable club from the USGA.

Until this year, Pelham Country Club was noted for two things: hosting perhaps the most exciting PGA Championship playoff ever contested; and watching the most heavily trafficked highway in America get routed through the middle of its golf course in the 1950s. But now it has the chance to be known for something entirely different: one of the most successful major golf course renovations in the Met Area.

The club, founded in 1908, has turned its swampy flood plain property into an award-winning modern ecological triumph, saving millions of gallons of treated water while keeping millions more of urban runoff from polluting Long Island Sound. In the process, nearly every hole on the course was rethought, with fourteen of them re-sequenced, several of those remodeled, and three built completely new.

Pelham Country Club's journey began with a predecessor club of the same name founded in 1898 with a nine-hole golf course on the other side of Boston Post Road. When the club was forced to move in 1904, a group of members migrated to New Rochelle and founded Wykagyl Country Club while others acquired the current property in 1908 and opened the new Pelham Country Club's first eighteen-hole course in 1921.

At about the same time the club made a significant statement by hiring "Long Jim" Barnes to be its head pro. Barnes had won the first PGA Championship, played at nearby Siwanoy CC in 1916, the next PGA in 1919 at Engineers on Long Island, and proceeded to win the US Open at Columbia Country Club in Maryland not long after his first day at Pelham CC. President Warren G. Harding presented Barnes with the winner's trophy on the eighteenth green in Chevy Chase.

Historic championship

Barnes was still playing out of Pelham when the club hosted the 1923 PGA Championship. Gene Sarazen and Walter Hagen met in the match-play finals in what could be termed the sport's first heavyweight title bout. The two were rivals of the first order. Sarazen, the son of Italian immigrants, started in the game as a caddie at The Apawamis Club up the road in Rye. Hagen, ten years older than Sarazen, began as a caddie as well, and went on to popularize the professional game. Known as a great showman, he was the first golfer to earn a million dollars in his career. Hagen, who had won three straight Met Opens, took his first of five PGA Championships in 1921 at Inwood. Sarazen, later a Met Open winner as well, won the PGA in 1922 at Oakmont when Hagen did not compete.

Hagen breezed into the finals, winning some of his matches by scores like 10 & 9 and 12 & 11 (in the semifinals!). Sarazen survived a tough battle in the quarterfinals with Jim Barnes on the latter's home turf, emerging with a 1-up victory. The two were even after the morning round, but Sarazen rode two birdies and a Hagen bogey to a 3-up lead after seven holes in the afternoon. But Hagen chipped away with birdies of his own, and when Sarazen bogeyed sixteen and seventeen the match was again all square after 36 holes, shifting the event into sudden death. They halved the 37th hole with birdies. The second (38th) hole, which was later buried when the New England Thruway was built, was a short dogleg left on the edge of the property. Both players tried to cut the corner; Hagen put his tee shot into a bunker 20 feet from the green, and Sarazen hooked his drive into the rough some 50 feet away.

Hagen suggested that Sarazen's ball was out of bounds, but they found it in the tall grass near the greenkeeper's house. Hagen joked that he could tell the ball had gone through a window and been tossed back out by the Italian residents because it was stained with spaghetti sauce. Sarazen laughed off the comment, turned to the crowd, and then called his shot, saying, "I'm going to put this so close it will break Walter's heart." He pitched out of the rough to two feet and made the birdie putt to close out the match after Hagen left his bunker shot in the sand. The club memorializes the match each year with the Sarazen Member-Member Tournament.

Re-imagining the golf course

Neither Sarazen nor Hagen would recognize today's golf course. The Devereux Emmet design they played underwent a severe overhaul when construction of I-95 took a significant slice of property along the railway line that bisects the course. Emmet's protégé Alfred Tull was called in to build replacement holes that opened in 1955. (Only two of Emmet's original holes are still in play—today's eleven and fourteen.) Aside from some work by Stephen Kay in the early 1990s, that was the last time the course was altered, but not the last time it would need alteration. The highway construction and subsequent commercial and residential development around the golf course exacerbated water problems the club simply lived with until the decision was made to fix them.

That major renovation was completed last year. "The area where we did the bulk of the work lies in a basin that was probably a boggy, marshy area before the course was built," explains Pelham CC board member Bruce Dunbar, who, with greens and golf co-chair Gary Coleman, spearheaded the project over the last decade.

"We wanted to find a way to collect irrigation water in a new pond," says superintendent Jeff Wentworth, who has been tending the course since 1994. "Digging the pond would generate a tremendous amount of earth, so we had to figure out a way to use it. It made sense to put it on the low-lying holes in the middle of the course." The club was buying as much as ten million gallons of potable municipal water every year. The course also was periodically awash in runoff from the urban watershed surrounding the club, which fed millions of gallons from parking lots and streets across the golf course, into Burling Brook, and eventually into Long Island Sound.

The renovation plan grew from the club's need to deal with its water issues, but it soon took on an even wider scope. "To be blunt," says Dunbar, "we had an outdated and hard-to-maintain piece of property. A course that was old-school, with three sets of tee boxes, none particularly friendly to ladies, seniors, or juniors."

Architect Mike DeVries, designer of a World Top 100 course (Cape Wickham) and one in the top 100 in America (Kingsley Club), had previously completed renovations at Sunningdale and Siwanoy in Westchester. He started working with Pelham about ten years ago, building a short game area with three practice greens that flow into the first tee. Two years later, the club adopted a master plan he presented and began addressing the problems on the course in stages.

The initial phase updated the seventeenth green and expanded the tee box and green for the par three eighteenth hole, along with dredging the pond that fronts it. Next came the conversion of the first hole from an anemic par five to a long par four with a more accessible green for golfers who need to run the ball in. Moving the first green allowed for creation of an additional short-game instruction area at the end of the range. Each job was separated by about two years, which meant the members had time to absorb the changes, Wentworth explains: "We wanted to give the members a break so we weren't just under constant construction."

In 2019, the major third phase began on terrain DeVries says may be the most difficult he's ever tackled. It wasn't easy—at one point, a Caterpillar excavator tipped over and almost sank into oblivion in the muck. It took three days to rescue it. An entirely new creek system was conceived; one pond was expanded and another one built from scratch, and several acres of wetland were created to capture more runoff. The course can now store over four million gallons of water, so it no longer needs municipal water for irrigation. The earth displaced by digging the water features was used to raise the level of the fairways in the lowest-lying part of the course.

All this work led the club to significantly improve the overall golf experience by building new holes and renovating others while also re-routing much of the course. "Our key feature is Mount Tom, the big rock in the middle," Wentworth says. "With the new routing, you see Mount Tom early in the round, play around it, then return to it later in the round. The holes we renovated were the five weakest holes. Now you could argue that they're the five best holes on the golf course."

The most memorable of the new holes are the third and fourth—a monster par five followed by a devilishly-inviting short par four. The 605-yard third features a series of strategically placed fairway bunkers, out of bounds right, and a green that's easily missed. The 273-yard fourth dares you to drive its narrow green. The approach is protected by a mound that rises across the front and makes the tee shot semi-blind for added entertainment. A moderate 240-yard drive will carry the top of the mound and might roll onto the green, while a 270-yarder will reach the front on the fly. If either one is off line by a yard or two, trouble awaits in greenside bunkers and deep swales on either side of the green.

Replacing the seriously flawed dogleg thirteenth hole (in the old routing) with the drive-able fourth was quite controversial. "There was a love-hate relationship with the old thirteenth hole," DeVries says. "Some people felt it was classical, unique, unusual in that most players had to hit a longer club for their second shot than they did from the tee. But it was not a safe hole. The residential properties along the right side were in danger from the second shot, and guys who wanted to cut the corner had to bomb one right over the old tenth green where people were putting. And there were a bunch of trees next to the green ricocheting balls."

Pelham member Mark Broadie, author of *Every Shot Counts*, provided data on shot dispersion that showed less danger to the adjacent residences from the new hole because the green is now farther from them and play is at a different angle. DeVries adds, "It's a fun hole that provides a lot of options for people."

"Fun" provides the subtext for much of the renovation. The course was made both longer and shorter to provide opportunities for every caliber of player to make par. From the back tees, it was stretched from 6,388 yards to 6,501. The forward tees, though, went from 5,552 to 5,218, and a fourth set of tees was added in between. That's not the only way the course was made more user friendly, according to DeVries: "In general, we tried to provide more open approaches for shorter-hitting players so they have the option to roll the ball up. There's more short grass in the surrounds, too, so the higher-handicap player doesn't always have to chip or pitch out of long rough."

Environmental benefits

The renovation gave the club another way to have a positive impact on the environment.

Wentworth says, "I did a bunch of research and picked two bent grass cultivars that were bred at Rutgers specifically to have a resistance to dollar spot. I believe we were the first golf course to plant it. Between our tees and our fairways, we're using 25-30% less fungicide versus the old turf. I think it will be even less going forward."

The cumulative effect of the club's earth-friendly approach earned it the 2020 Arthur P. Weber MGA Club Environmental Leaders in Golf Award, presented annually to a club for distinguished environmental leadership.

One of the club's most important assets – besides its modernized golf course and improved tennis, pool, and dining facilities—can be found every day in the pro shop. Head professional Mike Diffley has been setting high standards at Pelham since 1988. He is known throughout the Met Area as an outstanding player as well as an expert coach of the mental game. "Mike's contribution to the club is immeasurable," says Dunbar. "He manages to be a man of the people and a pro's pro at the same time. He's a great ambassador for the club and a great player. To have someone of his stature in the game at Pelham says a lot about the club."

Diffley earned his place in the local record books long before he joined the club. A graduate of St. John's University, he won the Metropolitan Intercollegiate Championship, led his team to the 1982 Big East Conference championship, and was one of two golfers chosen for the school's Athletic Hall of Fame. He won the 1982 Ike Championship, turned pro, and played on mini-tours in Florida and South Africa. Diffley won the 1991 Met Open and followed it the next year with the Westchester PGA Championship. In 2013 he not only won the Met PGA Senior Match Play but was named Met PGA Teacher of the Year. In 2016, Diffley received the Horton Smith award (since re-named the PGA Professional Development Award) by the PGA of America in recognition of his contributions to golf education. He has coached winners at all levels of the game, including Danny Balin, Ryan McCormick, James Ondo, Mike Gilmore, Shaun Powers, Met Open winners Andrew Svoboda and Grant Sturgeon, and Symetra Tour winner Nannette Hill.

Diffley's deepest joy, though, comes from his accomplishments at Pelham. "I have a lot of pride in this club. I have so many good friends here," he says. "I try to be an ambassador for the club when I play in events, even when I teach and give seminars."

Gutting and reinventing a hundred-year-old golf course is a risky move, but the circumstances at Pelham Country Club called for bold and fearless action and the club pulled it off, winning accolades from its members for turning a so-so disjointed track into a fun and challenging course designed to entertain players of all capabilities. The club also won copious praise—and awards—for turning an ecological monstrosity into a model of planetary stewardship.

At the same time, Pelham preserved its place as a championship venue, a training ground for high-caliber players, and an exceptionally family-friendly club. Gary Merjian, who joined Pelham as general manager this year, points out that over two-thirds of the 560 members live in town. "They walk to the club!" he says. "They use it like their own backyard, which is what we want."

Mike Diffley sums it up: "Members belong to this club to enjoy it, to use it. They're here to have fun. It's a wholesome place."

Notable Holes

#4, 273 yards, par 4 - (2020) One of the most entertaining risk and reward holes in Westchester is the new fourth at Pelham Country Club, a drive-able par four that even moderate strikers of the ball can reach from the tee. Early in your round you can card a birdie or even an eagle—or a bogey or worse—depending on how you manage the risks involved. The narrow green is protected by a substantial mound stretching across the front to make the tee shot semi-blind. Depending on the tee you play, your well-struck drive can carry the top of the hill and roll onto the green. A real bomb can reach the front on the fly. But if either tee shot is even a bit off line, it will end up in a greenside bunker or deep swale. A nicely safe par can be made with a 180-yard tee shot that lays up to the mound and leaves a simple wedge approach.

#18, 175 yards, par 3 - (2017) Par three holes aren't generally considered good closing holes, but the recently updated one-shot masterpiece at Pelham is the exception that proves the rule. The hole's constantly changing profile is what sets it apart. Depending on the wind speed, direction, and placement of the pin on the huge green on any given day, your tee shot can be played with any club from a hybrid to a wedge. Water is strongly in play in front of the green and on the left while a major league bunker guards the right.

PLEASANTVILLE COUNTRY CLUB
PLEASANTVILLE

Pleasantville

(2026) A century has passed since A.W. Tillinghast designed the nine-hole golf course for Pleasantville Country Club. Today the club offers a modern clubhouse (built in the 1990s) that includes a fitness center and locker rooms, while the course has added a teaching area and practice green. There's also tennis and a swimming pool. It's a casual but dynamic club with a full schedule of events and competitions.

POUND RIDGE GOLF CLUB
POUND RIDGE

Pound Ridge #2 (JF)

Grand Opening of a Grand Course (2008)

Pound Ridge Golf Club, Pete Dye's newly-opened ball-eater, is a spectacular golf course in a place where there are many spectacular golf courses already—Westchester County. His first New York course joins a pantheon of legendary tracks like Winged Foot, Quaker Ridge, Westchester Country Club, Fenway, and Century, not to mention legends-in-the-making such as Hudson National, GlenArbor, Golf Club of Purchase, Trump National, and Anglebrook. It will be interesting to see how it rates with this sophisticated golf community.

I toured Pound Ridge while it was under construction, then played it during the Grand Opening just before it went live to the public. Its look is unlike that of any other course in the area, which is what you would expect from Pete Dye and his son, Perry, who actually deserves most of the credit for the layout. The new course was literally blasted out of Westchester granite on 172 wooded, rolling acres. Fairways are narrow and undulated, surrounded my moguls, expansive bunkers, and what seems like miles and miles of stone walls (they had to do something with all that blast debris). Rock outcroppings are everywhere, as are environmentally-protected wetlands and acres of dense woodlands. The course is visually stunning.

At 7,171 yards from the tips, it's plenty of golf course, too, although four other sets of tees ranging down to 5,180 yards make it perfectly playable for all types of golfers. The key to enjoying the course, in fact, is choosing the right set of tees. Several holes have forced carries and obstacles like trees and rock formations that will ruin the round of the player who insists on playing the blues (6,787) when their handicap calls for the whites (6,279). That's a common theme, of course, but Pete Dye drives the point home with a vengeance.

**Pete Dye at Pound Ridge
Opening Day**

The eighteenth hole is the most controversial in that regard. From the white tees, it's a 415-yard par four with a series of bunkers along the left leading to a pond that pinches the front of the green. Moguls line the right side the length of the hole. Two huge maples stand 130 yards from the tee in the right rough. Go forty yards back to the blue tees, though, and the hole not only becomes a more respectable 454-yarder, but those two maples now completely block the line to the fairway about 170 yards off the tee. Since they're at least 75 feet tall, it's almost impossible to hit a driver high enough to carry over them. A sweeping fade means you have to aim directly at the fairway bunkers on the left; setting up for a draw points you at the adjacent fairway and has to come back over the moguls in the right rough.

As Dye told my friend John Paul Newport of the *Wall Street Journal*, "Anybody dumb enough to play the hole from back there can try to work around it if they want to. There'll be some bellyaching, but who cares?"

The most interesting feature of Pound Ridge, though, is that it's a daily fee course, not a private club. Owner Ken Wang, brother of fashion diva Vera Wang (who hits a mean driver herself, by the way) saw a need for a high-end public course in the New York metro market. He may be right, too, since Westchester County has a grand total of six public golf courses serving a population of nearly a million people. There are a few daily-fee courses within an hour's drive, but none of them are in the same league.

Five Years Later (2013)

Pound Ridge is D*&#%d hard! We all have "off" days on the golf course, but the last place you want to have one is at Pound Ridge GC, the Pete Dye design about an hour north of NYC. Show up with less than your "A" game and your ego will take quite a beating. The daily fee track is known for fabulous sculpturing of the land, majestic forests, and picturesque rock outcroppings, but it's always a good idea to keep Pete Dye's opening-day advice in mind: "Everyone agrees it's a beautiful piece of land. You just need to bring a lot of golf balls." If you can't hit it straight, you'll need a bucket full.

The first thing you discover at Pound Ridge is that precision isn't just nice to have, it's absolutely essential. Tee shots have to be not only in the fairway but in the right place in the fairway to have a shot at the green. Approach shots have to not only land on the green but end up in the correct place on the green to have a reasonable two-putt. Mistakes aren't just unfortunate, they're deadly. Off the fairway a yard or two? You'll be in four-inch rough with a wedge your best option. Miss it by ten yards or so? You've probably lost your ball in the fescue or one of the many, many environmentally-sensitive hazards. The same conditions apply, by the way, to most of the par threes.

That's not to say Pound Ridge isn't an enjoyable golf experience—just be mentally prepared for a tough round. The course is visually stunning, with 14,000 linear feet of rock walls, dramatic bunkering, and gorgeous water hazards. The green complexes have none-too-subtle but perfectly puttable contours, well-placed but playable traps, and numerous pin positions to keep things interesting from round to round. The turf and putting surfaces are as good as any private club--and better than many.

Pete Dye pointedly built five sets of tees with large differences not just in length of hole but angles of play, forced carries, and even hazards and obstacles between them. Choosing the correct tee is essential if you want any hope of playing a successful round. The tale is in the course rating for each tee, not the yardage. The "Oak" tees, for example, play 6,773 yards, a not-unplayable distance for many decent golfers using modern equipment these days. The course rating from those tees, though, is 73.8. That means a scratch golfer is expected to score nearly two over par if he shoots to his handicap that day!

The course isn't a pushover from the next set of tees forward, either. The "Granite" tees measure 6,261 yards with a 70.4 rating and 140 slope. From there, you'll face 200-yard-or-so carries off the tee on a couple of holes (nine and fourteen), not to mention the need to shape your tee shots on a couple more (ten and eighteen). Approaches over water will affect your strategy on the second and possibly the eighteenth hole. Elevated greens add to the difficulty on nine, thirteen, and sixteen.

Regardless of the tees you play, a house-size boulder, aka "Pete's Rock," sits in your line off the tee on the thirteenth hole, a 448-yard par five (from the Granite tees). The glacial erratic draws a great deal of commentary, but it also distracts from the real difficulty of the hole, which is lined by hazards on both sides of the narrow fairway all the way to the green. Golfers befuddled by the rock are much more likely to lose a ball right or left than to bounce one off the boulder. Even if your drive finds the short grass, your second shot needs to be laser-straight even if you are laying up to the long, narrow green.

Dye plays all sorts of mind games on the equally-infamous fifteenth hole, a relatively easy 144-yard par three. Once again, a granite outcropping immediately behind the green draws the player's attention while the hazard lining the front poses a much greater threat. The green is huge--some 60 yards wide--and set at an angle to the tee, so distance control is the key to par. Just to mess with you some more, though, Dye set the tees so that foliage in the hazard typically blocks your view of much of the putting surface.

Pound Ridge opened in 2008 to great acclaim and much comment about both its demanding layout and equally-demanding greens fees, which were easily the highest in the metro area. Deep-pocketed golfers flocked to the course, however, and owner Ken Wang's $40-million gamble appears to be paying off.

Notable Holes

#14, 401 yards, par 4 – (2010) Pound Ridge has many pleasures that are secrets simply because the course has only been open since 2008. This hole is one of the most intimidating Pete Dye delights you'll find anywhere. It all depends on which tees you play, of course, but this is one of the hardest driving holes you'll ever see—and that's meant literally, since you're faced with not one but two stone retaining walls on the other side of the water hazard you have to carry to reach the fairway, which is a full 222 yards uphill from the back tees. Even from the front tees where most bogey golfers should play, you'll need to carry your drive over 200 yards if it's aimed slightly too far left. And that's just to reach the other side! If you hope to see the green for your second shot, you'll need to drive the ball well.

#2, 451 yards, par 4 - (2023) A pond protects the green on the excruciatingly hard 2nd hole at Pound Ridge, so second-shot layups are the norm rather than the exception. You can still get your par, though, if you chip or pitch your approach shot with finesse. Head pro Brad Worthington says preparation for the shot is essential. He asks himself, "Is the ball sitting up or down in the grass? If it's sitting down I'll play the ball back in my stance and account for more run. Where do I want the ball to land? On an upslope or a downslope?" When it comes to technique, he says, "I set up with 80% of my weight on my lead leg. For the backswing I simply lift the club with my trail elbow, and for the downswing I pivot toward the target and extend my arms. Since my arms are not over-accelerating relative to my body, each pitch comes out high and lands softly. A successful shot rolls slowly and finishes close to the pin."

GOLF CLUB OF PURCHASE
PURCHASE

(2025) Perhaps the biggest renovation for 2025 was done by the Golf Club of Purchase, where every tee box, bunker, and green was rebuilt, many fairways reshaped, and several holes completely re-thought under the guidance of architect Tom Fazio and his team.

"This golf course was designed to be hard," says Director of Golf Carl Alexander. "The greens were small, averaging only 5,000 square feet. Making them larger gives us more hole locations. At the same time, it makes them more accessible. When people hit the green instead of a bunker, they have more fun."

At the same time, he says, "Challenging the better player in certain areas without penalizing the average player is one of our goals." It's a function of the passage of time, he says. "The new, younger members hit the ball a lot farther, so many of the bunkers are only capturing the older members' drives, so we're repositioning them."

One hole undergoing a major change is the fifteenth, a par five that required everyone but the longest drivers of the ball to hit a second shot layup to wetlands with a pitching wedge that then left them with a mid-iron into the green. Alexander explains, "We're moving the tee back and the green forward to flip that club selection. It's going to be a better hole."

Perhaps the biggest change is to the eighteenth hole. "You used to finish about 200 yards away from the clubhouse," he says. "We're bringing the green much closer. Among other things, that makes it visible from the patio for more social interaction."

Notable Holes

#7, 508 yards, par 5 - (2015) Carl Alexander, head pro at the Golf Club of Purchase, advises players to maintain their focus and not get distracted by the beautiful surroundings of the seventh hole, a three-shot par five. He also says, "This is no time to have negative thoughts. You must hit the shot you know you can. It doesn't have to be pretty, just in play." Avoiding penalty strokes may be the most important strategy for the bogey golfer on this hole. Alexander points out that hazards are a threat from the tee, so he suggests throttling back and swinging at about 95%. "Focus on solid contact and maintain your balance," he advises. A solid drive favoring the right side can carry the hazard and set up the next shot.

Your second shot is to a narrow landing area surrounded by wild environmental areas on both sides. Going for the green isn't really an option for the bogey golfer, so Alexander suggests choosing a hybrid to mid-iron in order to leave a comfortable distance into the green for the third shot. "You'll be playing into a green measuring just 14 paces wide at its narrowest point and 18 paces at the widest," he says, "and this shot must carry a rock wall that faces you in front of the green." There is a bank behind the green that can kick some balls back on the putting surface but any ball that stays up there is facing a tough chip back towards the hazard.

Alexander offers a final, encouraging word: "With a relatively flat green, once players find the putting surface they are rewarded with a good chance to make a putt."

#16, 435 yards, par 4 - (2023) Jack Nicklaus says he was inspired by the eleventh hole at Augusta when he designed this hole. A lake protects the left side of the green and, depending on your tee shot, you're challenging it with an approach shot that may need to fly 200 yards. There is a bail-out on the right side of the green, but it will leave you with a pitch back towards the lake. Director of golf Carl Alexander says, "The key to playing this hole is to keep your ball out of the penalty areas, right off the tee and left by the green. If you're out of position on the tee ball, playing short of the green is always an excellent choice to save par and avoid making more than bogey. Par is well-earned and often appreciated."

QUAKER RIDGE GOLF CLUB
SCARSDALE

Quaker Ridge #17 (JF)

Refresh and Renew (2022)

Like oil and water, technology and tradition seldom mix well, but at Quaker Ridge Golf Club they meld together perfectly. The 106-year-old Scarsdale club recently completed a multi-million-dollar clubhouse and pro shop renovation that added cutting-edge amenities to buildings that look like they've stood untouched for a century. The project reflects the membership's reverence for Quaker Ridge's place in metropolitan golf history as well as their desire to keep it relevant to future generations.

"The members are very loyal to the place and its history and love the people they associate with, both other members and staff," says club president Jeff Golenbock. "We did a survey asking what they wanted most and what we could improve and we built to their expectations."

Member expectations have always been high at Quaker Ridge, beginning with the founding of the club in 1916 by a group of highly successful New York businessmen led by William Rice Hochster. The 28-member group purchased a defunct nine-hole track in Scarsdale and immediately hired A.W. Tillinghast to build an eighteen-hole course that opened in 1918. Tillie was brought back in 1924 to expand the course onto an additional 28 acres purchased for that purpose. The rebuilt course opened for play in time for the 1928 Met PGA Championship, which was won by defending champion Gene Sarazen.

The course has won many kudos in the years since. One of the ingenious features of Tillinghast's design is the routing, which winds counter-clockwise around the periphery of the property for the first eight holes, connects the front and back nines with back-to-back par threes at right angles to each other, then follows the final eight holes basically clockwise through the interior. In a single round players will face every possible wind direction, not to mention elevation changes that angle fairways up, down, and sideways on the rolling terrain.

The golf course was updated most recently in a project begun in 2008 by Gil Hanse and has been continuously tweaked since. Hanse and his team made few alterations to the green complexes but many to the tees, bunkering, trees, and hazards to keep the course challenging for the modern long game.

The quality of the golf course helped make Quaker Ridge one of only three American clubs to host both the Walker Cup (1997) and the Curtis Cup (2018) matches. (Merion and Minikahda are the others.) This year, it will host the Covid-delayed French-American Challenge, the biennial competition between the MGA/WMGA and the Ligue de Paris.

Changes beyond the course

"We've done most of what we want to do with the golf course," says Golenbock, "and it's better than it's ever been." He adds, though, "There's been a change in lifestyle and we wanted a place people would find attractive and use even more." In 2018, the club began planning a major expansion and addition of amenities for the clubhouse and pro shop. "Our clubhouse was built in the 1920s, and while it was enhanced over the years, it was feeling its age." The Tudor-style clubhouse, designed by Buchman & Kahn, opened in 1923.

The project went into high gear in 2020 when the old golf shop was demolished and an all-new two-story building was erected in the same Tudor style. It features shopper-friendly retail space, dressing rooms, bag room, and staff offices on the first floor as well as outstanding displays based on the club's history. The most creative use of the additional space, though, was installation of three simulator-equipped hitting bays on that floor.

Once upon a time, clubs without driving ranges would have a net near the first tee so players could hit a few shots to warm up. Quaker Ridge has brought that concept into the 21st century. "Like many older clubs with limited land, we've always had to be creative about providing a range to warm up," says head pro Mario Guerra. "Now, the three downstairs bays in the golf center serve that purpose. When members and guest make a tee time, we book time before that for them in the bays so each person gets time to warm up." The hitting bays also open onto the first fairway for off-season use.

The second floor of the new building contains an irresistible party room with three more simulator bays, pool table, bar, lounge seating, and an indoor putting lab with an artificial green that moves to provide multiple contours and a computer system for measurement. All the simulators are powered by TrackMan, and the club made an additional investment: "We had the Quaker Ridge golf course rendered on the system," Guerra says. "Yes, you can play Pebble Beach and St. Andrews, but you can also play Quaker Ridge on the simulator. We can even give playing lessons inside! It's a tremendous asset."

The 30,000-square-foot clubhouse expansion project started as the golf center was being completed last year. The dining room and back terrace were taken down and a new entry foyer leading into a living-room-style history room were added. What used to be an outdoor terrace was enclosed and turned into an airy, high-ceilinged pub, a spacious drinking and eating space with bar, giant TV screens, and a welcoming convivial feel. The greatly enlarged dining room is extremely flexible, with two sets of glass doors that can be opened so that seating can be indoors, outdoors, or a combination of both environments at the same time. A large portion of the roof is retractable, too.

Additionally, the women's locker room was expanded, the grill room and men's locker room were refreshed, and a fitness center was added upstairs. "The fitness center is something we found people wanted when we did our survey," Golenbock says. "About half the club's members live in the city, so people come up for the day. Maybe they play golf or tennis or sit around the pool. The fitness center gives them another reason to use the club."

In another move to make the club even more usable, both the golf center and the clubhouse gym can be accessed by members using an app on their phones after hours or on days when the club is otherwise closed. They have access to their lockers, the fitness centers, and the simulators—all just about as easily as if all those amenities were in their home.

Honoring the past

The modernization and expansion of facilities was done with one eye on the future and the other on Quaker Ridge's storied past. Prominent members over the years included department store legends Franklin Simon, Samuel Bloomingdale, and Louis Gimbel, as well as Nathan Straus, founder of Abraham & Straus, who purchased Macy's and moved it to Herald Square. Another member of note was George Gershwin, who often invited his brother Ira to join him for a round.

Historic items displayed at Quaker Ridge

That past includes numerous Met Area championships held at Quaker Ridge. The club has hosted three Met Opens (1936, 1978, and 1993); the first was won by Byron Nelson, then a young assistant club pro playing out of Ridgewood CC, earning the first major victory of his professional career. Quaker Ridge was also the site of four Met Amateur Championships (1931, 1986, 1998, and 2010) and the 2004 Ike Championship. In addition to the 1928 Met PGA, the club has been the site for three others (1983, 1995, and 2009) as well as the Women's Met Open (1988 and 2003).

An important tradition at Quaker Ridge is the Hochster Memorial Tournament, first held in 1934, the year after William Rice Hochster died. The roster of Hochster competitors over the years gleams brightly: Willie Turnesa, who won a British and two US Amateurs and played on three Walker Cup teams, won the Hochster four times, as did Dick Siderowf and Jerry Courville, Sr. They were outdone by George Zahringer III, who took home the trophy six times. Golf Hall of Fame member Doug Ford, winner of the PGA Championship and the Masters, won the Hochster in 1946, the year before he turned pro. Freshman PGA Tour star Cameron Young won it in 2012.

Turnesa played another important role in perhaps the most impactful chapter in the club's history. He and long-time Quaker Ridge member Otto Reinach teamed up in 1956 to start what became the Westchester Caddie Scholarship Fund, which to date has granted $24 million in college scholarships to nearly 3,000 deserving young men and women.

The Quaker Ridge roster of golf professionals adds further luster to the club's legacy. The first was Jimmy Farrell, hired in 1919. He was joined as co-head pro the next year by his younger brother, Johnny, one of the leading playing pros of the day. Johnny Farrell won the Met Open in 1927 and defeated Bobby Jones in a 36-hole playoff at Olympia Fields to win the 1928 US Open Championship. He left Quaker Ridge for Baltusrol in 1934 after having won 21 PGA Tour events and competing in the first Masters. Jimmy Farrell stayed on until his death in 1939, when Vic Oberhammer took the helm and stayed there for 36 years.

Renowned instructor Jim McLean served as head pro from 1983-1986 and was followed by Rick Vershure, a perennial Met PGA and NY State PGA champion. Vershure held the position for 27 years. Mario Guerra stepped up to the head pro position at Quaker Ridge in 2018 after three seasons as a teaching assistant. Guerra spent six seasons at Sunningdale Country Club and taught at the Jim McLean School for many years, and has been recognized by *Golf Digest* as one of the Best Young Teachers in America.

The Quaker Ridge legacy has been enshrined throughout the clubhouse and golf center as an integral part of the building projects. Member Mark Hauser was asked early in the planning to spearhead the effort. "I found boxes of photos and magazines and memorabilia but needed help organizing and presenting the wealth of material, so I worked with long-time member Martin Davis and Andy Mutch, a professional golf curator and former director of the USGA Museum."

The club's members fully embraced the process. "Members would call and say they found a caddie jersey from the fifties, or their grandfather's clubs, or a hat with the old logo. It got wonderful support," Hauser says. Not everything could be placed on display, but the leftover materials are being catalogued and archived for future reference.

In a time when TrackMan generates the driving range and a cell phone unlocks the club's doors, history occupies an important place for the members of Quaker Ridge. Says Hauser, "You can't invent your history. In the world we live in today, authenticity is paramount. We took the club's legacy and put it on display."

The Curtis Cup (2018)

When the Curtis Cup brings sixteen of the world's best amateur women golfers to Scarsdale's Quaker Ridge GC June 8-10, the course will be ready for them. The biennial competition will be played on one of four A.W. Tillinghast courses within a ten minute drive that architect Gil Hanse has rejuvenated in recent history. Quaker Ridge, colloquially known as "Tilly's Treasure," will prove quite a test.

Hanse recently completed a multi-year restoration project of the two courses at Winged Foot GC, literally across the street from Quaker Ridge, and began one last year at Fenway GC not far away in Scarsdale. His work at Quaker Ridge was completed in 2008.

Curtis Cup play on Quaker Ridge #6

"This golf course requires you to be patient and figure it out," Hanse said. "It's all about angles and strategies. When golfers walk off the greens here with a par four, they'll be delighted because par is going to win a lot of golf holes." That's different from the usual go-for-broke mindset of match play, which prompted Hanse to opine that Quaker Ridge may not be a great match play course, although that depends largely on how the USGA sets it up.

Shannon Rouillard, the USGA's director of women's events, says "This match is going to be won or lost on the putting greens."

Virginia Grimes, the USA Curtis Cup Team captain, agrees: "I can't say enough about the greens." She points out that many of the women on the two teams don't often compete on heavily-contoured greens like those at Quaker Ridge, typical of many traditional northeastern US golf courses. When they are set up for tournament speeds with tight pins, scorecard havoc can quickly ensue.

The Curtis Cup pits a team of eight players from the US against one from Great Britain and Ireland. It's held every two years and has shone a spotlight on the early careers of Paula Creamer, Juli Inkster, Cristie Kerr, and Michelle Wie along with Stacy Lewis, Nancy Lopez, and Lexi Thompson.

Notable Holes

#9, 143 yards, par 3 - (2008) Aim counts on par threes, but distance control is paramount on the really good ones, like this short one-shotter that Jack Nicklaus reportedly said is harder than Winged Foot West's famed tenth hole. The triangular green is about the size of your dining room, with a back right shelf not much larger than a table for four that makes for one very devilish pin position. As Head Pro Rick Vershure explains, "Plenty of top players in the Hochster Memorial shoot for that pin and regret it. If they go long, it's almost impossible to chip back without running all the way down the steep green—and sometimes off the front into a bunker." The safe play is short, so you're well below the hole with a chance at making your long uphill putt.

#6, 434 yards, par 4 - (2015) Brian Gaffney, head pro at Quaker Ridge, has some solid advice for bogey golfers—and everyone else—faced with the innocent-looking sixth hole. "The trick to playing this hole is to do it very carefully," he says. "It's most important to keep the ball in play off the tee because there's a creek down the left side and rough on a steep hillside on the right. If you can get your ball into the fairway, the next challenge is to avoid the two bunkers that guard the left and right side of the hole on your second shot." That's where laying up might not be a bad idea. "If you can get past them in two," Gaffney says, "you should have a high percentage shot onto the green. Of course, then you have to putt on that green. It's amazing it's such an incredible design from 100 years ago. You can still one-putt for a par if you stay below the hole."

Quaker Ridge #14 (JF)

#14, 517 yards, par 5 - (2021) A.W. Tillinghast named this spectacular par five "Sahara" for a good reason and the Gil Hanse renovation made the sandy appellation even more apt by expanding the twenty bunkers that define the hole. The first two come into play off the tee, where your drive needs to stay between a big trap on the right side of the landing area and an even bigger one on the left, the first of eight sandy hazards on that side of the fairway. Then there are the five cross bunkers that force most players to lay up rather than chance reaching the green in two with an uphill blind shot than can easily end up in yet another bunker—there are four of them greenside as well as two right of the fairway closer to the hole. Laying up has another advantage: you'll have a better chance with a wedge to find the right spot on the exceedingly complicated multi-level green.

#11, 372 yards, par 4 - (2006) A short, easy hole, as long as you can laser-guide your tee shot to the right third of the fairway and loft a high, soft iron over the creek to just the right spot on the green. The hole has two features that dictate pinpoint accuracy: the tree and the creek.

"If you hit your A-1 best tee shot and fit it in the right edge of the fairway, you can get an angle around this ninety-foot tulip tree at the green," advises head pro Rick Vershure. Then, he says, "From eighty yards and in, the creek is all over the place. It's left, front, right. It's kind of snaking around in front of the green and looking for you." Even as short as the hole is, many players lay up to the treacherous stone-lined creek with their second shot. If the pin is in the front, it's easy to spin the ball back into the creek.

RYE GOLF CLUB
RYE

Rye Golf #17

(2009) One of the best surprises I've had in a long time came when I played the Rye Golf Club for the first time in about five years. Since I was there last, the venerable municipal course has undergone some major revisions and taken giant leaps forward in conditioning. Now, I'd rank it among the best publicly-owned courses I've seen.

One of the unique features, as head pro Mike Rapisarda never tires of telling people, is that it is the only course in Westchester where you can hit a ball into Long Island Sound. In fact, there are two holes where that dubious feat can be accomplished. One is the 315-yard par four twelfth hole that just begs for a big hitter to drive the green, thereby bringing the sound into play on the left. The other is the tortuous par three seventeenth. The green is about the size of a dinner napkin and the wind can easily take your ball out to sea if you're not careful.

The par 71 track was originally laid out by Devereux Emmet in 1921, but I don't imagine the old boy would recognize it today. The course has been stretched to 6500 yards, every tee and bunker has been rebuilt, the fairways converted to bent grass, and hundreds of trees have been taken down to open more of the course to those wonderful Sound views. All of the work, by the way, has been designed and carried out by Superintendent Chip Lafferty, who came to the course in 2003.

The course is owned by the City of Rye, NY, and is open to members and their guests. I recommend you find a member and beg an invitation.

SALEM GOLF CLUB
NORTH SALEM

Salem #13 (JF)

Shape Shifting Always to the Better (2020)

A sense of relief prevails on the ninth tee at Salem Golf Club. You've survived the gauntlet through the valley where you faced down the elevated monster of a three-tier green on the soul-crushing par five third hole. You finessed your tee shot to set up your favorite wedge distance over the water on the 300-yard dogleg sixth. Now, on the ninth, the fairway seems wider, the sky bluer as you play back up the ridge toward the classic clubhouse.

That feeling of relief is a delusion. The back nine plays just as hard as the front and requires the same mix of power and accuracy. Your tee shot on the short eleventh hole can go wrong in every conceivable way—in the water, out of bounds, too short so you're blocked for your approach or too long so you have to put spin on an uphill wedge out of the rough. The thirteenth hole has similar threats off the tee with the added danger of three church-pew bunkers you must avoid to reach the two-club uphill green with your blind second shot.

In other words, the golf course is a blast. Making and keeping it that way hasn't been easy either agronomically or financially.

Staying economically viable in the golf industry is no easy feat these days. For the last three decades, Salem GC has accomplished that by anticipating lifestyle changes and creating new amenities and membership packages to meet them. Club ownership has been willing to ignore social conventions in order to attract a diverse membership and hire the best staff without regard to industry stereotypes. The club has also been an early adopter of technology and modern agronomy practices.

Perhaps most importantly, Salem's owners have consistently invested serious money in the facility—even in times of economic distress—to keep the golf course in championship shape and relevant to today's game.

Taking chances

Among the many game-changing decisions the club has made over the years was appointing the first female head golf professional at a private club in the region, Kammy Maxfeldt, in 1995 and keeping her there until 2003. Maxfeldt won the Met Women's Open in 1997 while managing golf operations at Salem. The club also made national headlines in 2001 when it offered to admit Bill Clinton as a member after reports surfaced that he had been turned away by several other clubs in Westchester as he prepared to leave office.

The prime mover and chief change agent at Salem is the managing partner of the non-equity club, Joel Berman, an attorney and real estate investor who didn't even play golf when he acquired the property in 1983. "I bought the club as a real estate investment," Berman explains. "Instead, I fell in love with the game and the club and it became part of my life." Out of curiosity, Berman took some lessons from Salem's pro at the time, John Leathers, and the hook was set.

Berman and his partners bought Salem GC from the Lawrence Investing Corporation, which had built the course in 1966 on a 165-acre dairy farm it purchased from the Nichols family of Camden, N.J. The Nichols clan spent summers in North Salem and built their getaway home, "Bluebird Cottage," in 1905; today it forms the heart of Salem's clubhouse.

Lawrence retained local golf architect Ed Ryder to create the layout on the rolling landscape. Ryder had just completed the back nine at Morefar Golf Club in nearby Brewster, N.Y., in 1964, and would go on to build Richter Park Golf Course in 1972 in Danbury, Conn. He routed the Salem course along two plateaus, with thirteen holes on higher ground and five on lower. The front nine includes the lower five holes and plays very differently from the back side, which offers some spectacular vistas. With holes winding through wetlands and woodlands and farms surrounding the property, the course is home to an active and visible wildlife population.

"The golf course was in pretty decent shape when I bought it," Berman says, "although it didn't have an irrigation system, so one of the first things we did was to put one in." Since then, the course infrastructure has been continually improved. In 2019 they started installing a subsurface system built by XGD to improve green drainage.

Golf is front and center

"The golf course is primary," Berman explains. "We're up against the Winged Foots, Old Oaks, Century, and other top clubs, so the competition is tough here." He says every hole on the course has been touched in some way. Bunkers have been completely upgraded three times, new ones added, and many moved to match the modern game. New tee boxes have stretched the course to 6800 yards, from which it carries a hefty 73.5 Course Rating and 139 Slope. Two other sets of tees at 6500 and 5700 yards make the course playable for normal people.

Salem #11 (JF)

"The golf course is highly varied," according to superintendent Tom Reyes, who joined the staff from Century CC in 2019. "There are a lot of elevation changes and we've done a lot of tree work to reclaim many of the impressive views." He estimates they've removed 500 trees in the last three years. "I like the fifth, sixth, and seventh holes; it's pure golf. It's a different look because you're in a valley looking up at trees. When you come over to the peak of the course looking down from fourteen, it's different."

Adds head professional Charlie Poole, a 17-year veteran of the club, "The course plays very differently depending on the wind and weather. I can play the ninth hole with a driver and a four iron or driver and wedge. You can play this course every day without ever getting tired of it."

"Since 2004, we've invested over $15 million in this place. Whatever needs to be done gets done," Berman declares. Investment decisions, he adds, are based on the combination of a viable business model and his passion for the game.

What they're not based on, he notes, are member group-think decisions. "One of the major benefits of being a privately-owned club is that you can do things without a committee," he says. "When you have equity ownership, you have management by committee. There are too many arguments. The younger members want everything changed immediately, while the older ones don't want anything changed. Club boards can also get very political. We don't have any of that."

What do members get in return for not having the privilege of voting? "When the club is privately owned, there's no sales tax on dues," Berman says. "There's also never been an assessment on members in the 36 years I've owned the club. You pay your dues and that's it." A full family membership is $12,500 and includes kids up to age 24. Individual golf memberships are $10,000.

Other investments Berman and his partners have made in the club include one of the first comprehensive short game practice areas in Westchester County (added in 2004); a 15,000-square-foot extension to the clubhouse that same year that included a 230-seat dining room, fieldstone verandas, and expansive new locker rooms; and in 2018, a pool and pool house with gym, golf simulator, children's room, full kitchen, and outdoor patio. Coming this year is an entirely new fleet of GPS system-equipped carts that will automatically keep golfers out of prohibited areas and allow the pro shop to monitor every foursome's position on the course. While there is a limited caddie program at the club, most members ride.

Changing market

These investments have kept Salem ahead of the curve in meeting the demands of a changing marketplace. "Everyone comes here for a different reason," says general manager Melissa Sears. "The club to them may be about golf with the guys, or as a place to entertain clients, or they want to teach their kids to play golf the same way their father taught them. Lately I get more questions about, 'What else do you offer?' Our amenities are what really sell memberships right now. Everyone wants to know what they're getting for their membership dollar."

Aggressive membership recruitment has always been a hallmark of Salem's success, according to Berman: "We were perhaps the first club to have special membership prices for young professionals and seniors. We've innovated membership categories consistently." As of this writing, Salem offers six membership categories that include various levels of access to facilities and activities. It also offers to customize packages for individual prospects and even re-package features for existing members.

"The biggest change we've seen is that our golfer doesn't join the club by himself," Sears says. "Their spouse may be a social member or use the pool or fitness center. The member may have been here for 25 years, but now his older children are becoming members. The father is the legacy member but his children are coming with their children. Our membership categories need to include those changes."

Every club pursues millennials, Berman points out, but the other end of the age spectrum is living longer, which makes seniors a profitable market segment if you can retain them. "They may want to stay at the club, but can no longer afford it," he says. "Or they're living in Florida or the Carolinas most of the year, but are here in the summer. You have to accommodate these different categories."

Sears adds, "Our Sports membership lends itself to serving the needs of the aging golfer, who may not play as much as he or she used to, but still wants to be involved with the club and the game. They still enjoy all aspects of club life like the social events and dining with their friends, and don't have to leave just because it doesn't make sense to spend a lot of money for golf privileges that they won't use as often as they used to."

Such non-traditional memberships are where Salem has seen substantial success. "Our family sports membership allows you to be a pool member but be able to purchase rounds of golf," Sears says. "We've found that people convert into full golf members after they try it a few times. Sports members can purchase one round of golf per month at $150 ($125 weekdays) including cart. Family sports membership dues are $3,700. The family sports membership is also a good intro for people who didn't grow up with a country club in their life. They can afford a pool membership and get enticed into golf when they're around it."

The investment in club amenities lets Salem stage some attractive members-only events that enhance the value of social memberships. "We have become an activity center for people in town," Sears says. "A lot of our local residents take advantage of our social memberships, and many of our events sell out." One of the most popular is a progressive wine dinner the club introduced two years ago. "We're using our golf course for something other than playing the game: We take our guests out on the course in carts with lanterns to dine while watching the sunset."

A willingness to innovate in anticipation of market trends and to make continuous capital improvements to the vital center of the club—its golf course always, its other amenities more recently—have made Salem GC a flexible and successful business built on member satisfaction. "The club has changed remarkably since we bought it," Berman says. "The nature of the whole club is constantly changing to show a new face to everyone and keep the place growing."

Notable Holes

Salem #14 (JF)

#14, 595 yards, par 5 - (2009) It's a solid 350 yards to the hard left turn in the dogleg on this fascinating hole, so don't even think about reaching the green in two unless you have a PGA Tour card and your name is Bubba. Just relax and pound one down the hill somewhere in the center of the nice wide fairway, then decide how daring you want to be for your second shot, which can be anything from a short iron over the trees to a hybrid hooked around them. The idea, according to Head Professional Charlie Poole, is to "Make your birdie the old-fashioned way—with a wedge." You'll have to fly that wedge approach over the pond fronting the green, so choose your lay-up distance accordingly.

#13, 407 yards, par 4 - (2021) The thirteenth hole at Salem epitomizes the club's commitment to continual improvement. Over the years, the water hazard on the right has expanded, the woods and wetlands on the left have been groomed, and church pew bunkers have been added in front of the green to make it one of the most difficult second shot holes in the county. Most recently, tree removal made it more tempting for big hitters to boom one off the tee, but recontouring of the fairway line brought the hazards more into play on both sides of the fairway.

SAXON WOODS GOLF CLUB
SCARSDALE

Saxon Woods #1

(2010) Did legendary golf architect A.W. Tillinghast (Winged Foot, Quaker Ridge, Bethpage, Baltusrol, etc.) design Saxon Woods? According to his records he did, although official credit is given to Tom Winton, a Scot who was the official golf architect for the Westchester Parks Commission and whose other credits include Mount Kisco Country Club and all the other county courses except Dunwoodie.

There are many Tillinghast trademarks on the course. The third hole, a long "three-shotter" as he would have called it, has an obviously artificial mound cramping the fairway at the landing area for the second shot as well as two steep-faced bunkers squeezing the green. The fifth hole, my favorite on the course, is a dogleg par four that offers two strategies off the tee—a well-placed straight drive to the left half of the fairway that leaves a mid-iron over another mound, or a long fade to a narrow alley next to the mound that rewards the perfect tee shot with a wedge approach. The green, too, is highly contoured and protected by a bunker on the right. The sixteenth hole is one of the best par threes around, with a steep narrow green set at an angle. It's also surrounded by bunkers and fronted by a stream. The real Tilly touch is the tee box, which points not at the green but to the right of it.

Saxon Woods players this year should enjoy a substantially dryer round, as well as better bunkers and an entirely different sixth hole, thanks to a $4 million refurbishment of the course drainage system slated for completion during the winter.

SCARSDALE GOLF CLUB
HARTSDALE

Scarsdale #8 (JF)

Scarsdale GC, founded in 1898, is one of the oldest clubs in Westchester. The first course, a nine-hole track, was designed by Willie Dunn, and an additional nine holes were added two years later. A.W. Tillinghast recreated the course with seven new holes and many other changes that took effect in 1924. The club is noted not just for golf, but for a wide variety of winter activities including ice skating, sledding and even skiing. A group known as the "Scarsdale Snowbirds" plays the course year-round.

The course has been a qualifying site for the US Open and US Senior Open Championships as well as numerous MGA events. In 2010, Ralph Wimbish and Dave Donelson (the author of this tome), earned a place in MGA history with a victory in the eighteenth MGA Senior Net Four-Ball Tournament. The event, which was originally scheduled for May, was postponed twice due to rain and was finally completed on October 4. Wimbish and Donelson shot a 10-under-par 61 to finish one stroke ahead of their nearest competitors. The win marks the first MGA championship for the team as well as their club, the Quill & Tee, the official club of the Metropolitan Golf Writers Association.

Dave Donelson and Ralph Wimbish

Notable Holes

#1, 360 yards, par 4 - (2007) Staying out of trouble on the short opening hole on this A.W. Tillinghast gem is simple. All you have to do is fire a shot from the elevated tee that's not too short, not too long, not too far right, and not too far left. Actually, the ideal tee shot is 220 yards to a narrow neck of fairway. Drop yours there and you'll have 140 easy yards to the green.

Accuracy is called for because a lake lurks along the entire left side of the hole. Straight and long off the tee—normally a good thing—means you'll go through the fairway and land with a splash. So does short with a draw. Try to get cute and fade it right off the tee, and you're flirting with knee-deep fescue on a hillside only a mountain goat could love. It stretches the length of the fairway on that side. Even if you can find your ball in the rough, you'll have to hit it over or around a stand of trees that creates the neck in the fairway you were aiming for in the first place.

#7, 435 yards, par 4 - (2010) One of Westchester's newest golf pleasures is the seventh hole at Scarsdale, which opened in 2009. The old par five became a demanding par four during the rebuild, with a tough new green that was moved forward about eighty yards. The tee shot is blind, uphill, and generally into the wind, followed by an approach off a lie that's guaranteed to be anything but level. Regardless of the pin position, aim for the right side of the new green, since everything runs to the left, and check your distance, too, since a ridge across the green can leave you with a tricky downhill putt if you're not careful.

#8, par 4, 465 yards - (2025) A tender touch with a hybrid can bring a par on this long par four. Head pro Michael Docktor says it's possible to run the ball onto the green from the right side of the fairway or fly the bunker from the left side. "The main thing about hitting a hybrid," he says, "is to feel like you're sweeping the ball off the ground with a level swing and high follow-through."

SIWANOY COUNTRY CLUB
BRONXVILLE

Siwanoy #6 (JF)

125th Anniversary (2026)

Siwanoy Country Club honors its past this year while looking confidently into the future. The club has come a long way in the 125 years since it was founded in 1901 in Mount Vernon. The club moved to its current location in Bronxville ten years later and retained Donald Ross to design the golf course it plays today.

Perhaps the crown jewel of the club's history was the first PGA Championship, which was held by the newly-formed PGA of America in 1916. Siwanoy head pro Tom Kerrigan hit the opening drive. The closely-contested tournament was decided by a five-foot putt by "Long Jim" Barnes on the final hole.

Siwanoy has not rested on its laurels. About a decade ago, the original Donald Ross course underwent significant restoration by architect Mike DeVries. Several tee boxes were added, bunkering adopted to modern play, and extensive water management brought the classic course back to the original concept.

"Our membership has changed over the years," Freeman says. "It's much younger now than it used to be and that gives it a different perspective. About 75% of the membership is local, which makes Siwanoy a real community club with something for everyone in the family."

In addition to swimming and court sports, the club has a hockey rink for winter use and is building a new golf services facility with simulator bays, a training center, new golf shop, and a deck equipped with a bar. Freeman says, "We're really going to be even more of a twelve month club going forward."

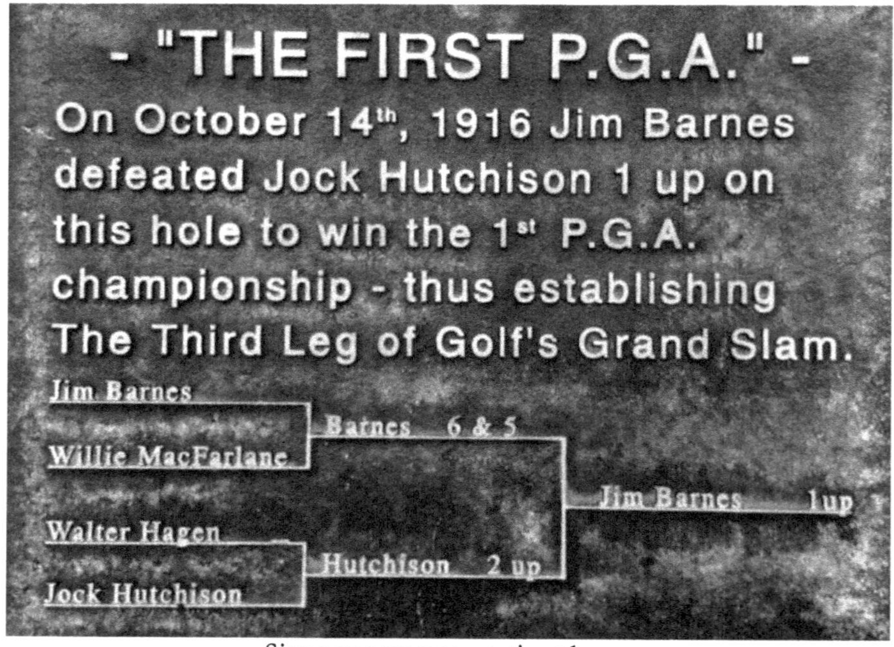

Siwanoy commemorative plaque

The First PGA Championship (2016)

The world's best golfers gather this week at Baltusrol to play the 100th anniversary edition of the PGA Championship. The very first one, though, was a Westchester affair contested at Siwanoy Country Club in Bronxville in 1916. It was a major tournament then as now, with more than 10,000 spectators turning out to watch Walter Hagen and other top pros compete for a purse of $2,580 donated by retailer Rodman Wanamaker.

Siwanoy CC celebrates the event this week with the Siwanoy Centennial Invitational, an outing laden with top PGA pros that will benefit the Metropolitan PGA Foundation. Participants include Larry Nelson, a three-time major championship winner; Rocco Mediate, who won the 2016 Senior PGA Championship and famously lost to Tiger Woods in the 2008 US Open; and multiple-time PGA Tour winners Jim Gallagher, Michael Bradley, Johnson Wagner, Olin Brown, and Will McKenzie. In addition to playing with the pros, attendees will see them compete in a long-drive contest using hickory-shafted clubs.

When the first PGA Championship was held, Siwanoy CC was already one of Westchester's leading clubs. Founded in 1901 by 107 members who paid a $10 initiation fee and $20 annual dues to belong, the club was originally located in Mount Vernon. It lost its lease there a couple of years later when the property was sold to a certain "Mr. Bailey," who owned a circus along with a partner named "Barnum." After a 10-year residence on another leased site in Mount Vernon, it found its permanent home in Bronxville on property that had been given by the Continental Congress to David Williams, one of the soldiers that captured Major Andre as he tried to help Benedict Arnold betray the fort at West Point to the British during the American Revolutionary War.

Donald Ross had advised the club on purchase of the property and designed today's eighteen-hole course. At the time, it measured less than 6,300 yards, which was short even for the day (today it stretches 6,617 from the tips). Ross's design, though, had elevated tees, brooks that wound treacherously through the fairways, and well-bunkered and heavily contoured greens.

The PGA of America was founded in April of 1916—its first president was Robert White, the head pro from Wykagyl Country Club in New Rochelle—and the first PGA Championship was held in October. Siwanoy head pro Tom Kerrigan hit the first shot in the 32-player field. The event was match play, with each pair going 36 holes per round, which meant the finalists spent five long days on the course.

The semi-finalists included three British-born professionals—"Long" Jim Barnes, a Philadelphia resident who eliminated Kerrigan in the quarterfinals, and Scots Willie MacFarlane and Jock Hutchison—and American Walter Hagen, who would go on to win 11 professional major titles, a total exceeded only by Jack Nicklaus and Tiger Woods. Hagen fell to Hutchison and Barnes beat MacFarlane, setting up the epic final match on Oct. 14.

Hutchison took a one-hole lead out of the morning round played in windy conditions that pushed both players to 77s—six strokes over par.

On the first tee after lunch, Barnes calmly pronounced, "I always do better after lunch," and proceeded to post a 2-up lead after the 28th hole. Hutchison rallied to go 1-up after the 33rd hole, and the match was all square when they teed it up on the 545-yard final hole. PGA Historian Bob Denney wraps up the tale: "Arriving on the eighteenth green, both players had five-footers for pars. After a measurement, it was determined that Hutchison was out. He missed his putt and Barnes made his, winning 1-up, a $500 prize, and a diamond medal."

Over the last two years, Siwanoy has undergone significant restoration by architect Mike DeVries. Several tee boxes were added, bunkering adopted to modern play, and extensive water management brought the classic course back to the original Donald Ross concept. One of the most interesting features is the expansive practice putting green just outside the clubhouse. It also seamlessly includes the first tee, which makes for fluid play and great views from the grill room.

Notable Holes

#6, 160 yards, par 3 - (2016) This devilish one-shotter received a complete makeover as part of the grand restoration of the 115-year-old club's Donald Ross course led by architect Mike DeVries over the last couple of years. "Great greens make great golf," DeVries says. "That's where the majority of the game is played and the green affects the angles and strategies of every shot." That's never been more true than on this gem, which requires pinpoint accuracy from an elevated tee to an elevated green to not only avoid the wicked bunkers but to land your ball below the cup—a must for a chance at par on the slick, strongly-contoured green.

#8, 340 yards, par 4 - (2020) Without a solid game plan, whatever can go wrong, will go wrong on the eighth hole at Siwanoy. Blasting a testosterone-fueled driver off the tee is fun, but that idea will probably leave you hitting your approach shot off a severe downslope into an elevated green, which isn't fun at all. Even with a level lie for your second shot, be careful about pin-seeking, especially if the cup is cut near the edges of the green where it usually is. A slight miss can send your ball into bogey territory in a heartbeat.

SLEEPY HOLLOW COUNTRY CLUB
SCARBOROUGH

Sleepy Hollow #16

Centennial Celebration (2011)

Sleepy Hollow Country Club celebrates its 100th anniversary today. The club was founded by the nation's most prominent business leaders at the pinnacle of America's "Gilded Age," opening officially on May 20, 1911.

Sleepy Hollow will acknowledge its centennial with various activities, but top of the list is the Metropolitan Open, which will be played at the club for the first time since the tournament began in 1905. The Met Open is the MGA's premier event and one of the most prestigious tournaments in the nation. The championship title has been held by all-time greats of the game including Gene Sarazen, Byron Nelson, Walter Hagen, Henry Picard, Tommy Armour, Paul Runyan, Craig Wood, and Claude Harmon.

Bob Rittberger of Garden City CC is the defending champion for the 54-hole event to be held August 23-25 at Sleepy Hollow.

They will play on the only course in Westchester designed by Charles B. Macdonald. Over the years, the course has been changed for various reasons, but a major restoration was undertaken in 2007 under the architect's pen of Gil Hanse. The goal was not to rebuild Macdonald's original layout (which would have been impractical given all the changes the course has endured over the years) but to recreate a course blending Macdonald's concepts with the demands of the modern game. The results are generally spectacular.

When Sleepy Hollow opened in 1911, there were 600 members and a long waiting list. The founding members were a Who's Who of the business community of the day including John Jacob Astor (who died a year later on the Titanic), William Rockefeller (brother of John D. Rockefeller), and Frank Vanderlip (President of the National City Bank of New York, the forerunner of today's Citigroup). Vanderlip was the creator of the club, which he founded on property he bought from Rockefeller, who had himself purchased it from Margaret Louisa Vanderbilt Shepard, a granddaughter of Cornelius Vanderbilt.

The Sleepy Hollow clubhouse is as magnificent as the golf course. It was completed in 1895 at a cost of $850,000—a huge sum for the time—and retains today the original character and features of the design by architects McKim, Mead, and White. The mansion includes a ballroom, library, formal dining room, and 18 guest rooms as well as the golf pro shop and locker rooms. An original Tiffany window lights its grand staircase and the view of the Hudson River may well be the finest in the county.

Golf is not the only activity offered at Sleepy Hollow. A spectacular European-style stable is home to some 50 horses and is the centerpiece of the club's extensive equestrian program. There are also two indoor and two outdoor riding rings. Members can also indulge in swimming, tennis, skeet and trap shooting, and squash. Golf is king, however, with an additional nine-hole course and state-of-the-art instruction and practice facility also available.

Notable Holes

#16, 155 yards, par 3 - (2007) Sleepy Hollow, the only Westchester course designed by pioneering golf architect Charles Blair Macdonald, celebrates a glorious centennial in 2011. This hole, one of the most photographed holes in the Northeast, really came into its own following the 2006 renovation restoring it to Macdonald's style and standards. Assuming you can tear your eyes away from the magnificent view of the Hudson River beyond it, the green is an inviting forty yards wide. The size of the putting surface is deceiving, though, since the edges are shaved and the dramatic contours make for many downright cruel pin positions. Wind is a major factor too, of course, given the tee's place atop one ridge and the green's on another.

Sleepy Hollow #1 (JF)

#1, 418 yards, par 4 - (2024) Head Pro A.J. Sikula says the opener at Sleepy Hollow is "underrated as a risk and reward hole. Drives to the right of the fairway are safer off the tee because of the big fairway bunker on the left, but they leave a very tough angle into the green, particularly when the hole location is right front. The reward for challenging the left side off the tee is a slightly longer but better second shot."

#3, 160 yards, par 3 - (2008) "Don't slice, don't slice, don't slice" is the mantra chanted by players facing the third hole at Sleepy Hollow. Less famous than its photogenic brother, the sixteenth hole, the third presents its own challenge to those willing to risk firing at a pin anywhere on the right side of the green. Send your tee shot just a little bit more than you should in that direction and you'll land in the greenside bunker—if you're fortunate. Miss that particular trap, and your ball is headed for the bunker below it, where you'll be lucky to see the flag, much less the hole. If you get a bad bounce, you'll be trying to get up and down from the valley of doom—not a place you want to play from.

Sleepy Hollow #18 (JF)

#18, 426 yards, par 4 - (2017) Perhaps the most intimidating part of the uphill finisher at Sleepy Hollow is the prospect of ending your round under the bemused eyes of the gallery that always seems to congregate on the terrace overlooking the green. If you keep your mind on your approach, though, play to the left side of the green to avoid the nasty bunkers on the right, and take an extra club to compensate for the elevation change, you should be able to close out your round with a par and a sigh of relief before you join the gang on the terrace to watch the next group play the hole.

 # 8, 460 yards, par 4 - (2021) There's no road near the "Road" hole at Sleepy Hollow, but Gil Hanse modeled it after the famous seventeenth hole at Saint Andrews in Scotland, with a menacing bunker that swallows errant approach shots that miss short and left of the newly-contoured and re-shaped green. Plenty of errant shots are made, too, especially since the fairway's many humps and bumps have been liberated by improved fairway turf conditions that catch even the best of drives and leave the player with an uneven stance for the next shot. The fairway now plays hard and fast thanks to removal of hundreds of trees that weren't in play but restricted airflow to the grass.

Sleepy Hollow #12 (JF)

#12, 536 yards, par 5 - (2020) What looks like a simple par five is much more complex than you think, according to head pro David Young. "There are three ways to play this interesting par five," he says. "If you've hit a good drive, you can always go for the green in two. It's elevated, though, and the green itself has a couple of shelves, so you will want to make sure of the pin position if you want to get close. The second option, hitting your second shot short of the creek, will have much less risk. It's a big green, so again, check the pin position to decide what distance you want to leave for your approach. Finally, many players don't realize there is a lay-up area left of the creek which gives a good angle into the green for your third shot."

SOMERS NATIONAL GOLF CLUB
SOMERS

(2022) When new owners took over the former West Hills Course in Heritage Hills in 2019, they promised to renovate the hilly, sub-par facility and present a public-golf alternative worthy of play in golf-rich Westchester. Their goal was achieved with Somers National GC, an interesting track where local knowledge helps a lot and a steady hand on the putter is needed to put pars on the scorecard. Somers National rewards the player who takes time to study the options on each hole before bombing away with the driver off the tee. The 389-yard 3rd hole, for example, lets you choose whether to challenge the water on the left or the trees on the right with your tee shot. The 628-yard, par five fourteenth hole features a fairway that bends like a snake before bringing you to a tiny green protected by a creek. It's fun golf and not for the faint of heart. The semiprivate club offers memberships, as well as daily-fee play.

SPRAIN LAKE GOLF CLUB
YONKERS

Sprain Lake #9

(2010) When the county opened Sprain Lake Golf Course in 1929, it was billed as "an island of green space" next to Grassy Sprain Reservoir and one of the most densely populated parts of the county. The course is short, but plays tougher than it looks, at least the first time you challenge its quirky fairways and small, highly-contoured greens. Local knowledge is the key to scoring on this course. Placement off the tee and keeping your ball below the hole on your approaches matter a whole lot more than how far you can bomb your driver.

In fact, many players won't take their driver out of the bag at all until they reach the par five tenth hole, but that doesn't mean they won't have challenges on the front nine. Position in the fairway matters a lot at Sprain, particularly on the blind third hole and dogleg seventh, where a long-straight drive will go through the fairway and into the water. Length matters a little more on the back, but even there an off-line drive will add more than a stroke on the thirteenth, fifteenth, and seventeenth holes. The only hole where a long, long drive makes a difference is number eighteen, a 440-

yard par four. Even there, your tee shot should be on the left half of the fairway for the best angle into the tiny green.

(2013) Sprain Lake is unique in that your tee shot will likely determine your score on almost every hole. Most courses put greater emphasis on the approach shot, but this Tom Winton design rewards the player who puts the ball in the fairway on their first shot by allowing for simple approaches to the generally accessible greens.

That's not to say the 6,110-yard par 70 layout is a complete pushover. Those tee shots require more than just a good wallop with a driver. In fact, even when you do use the big stick off the tee, you need to shape your shot with a fair degree of finesse to keep the ball on the short grass. Fairways are narrow, many of them are tree-lined, and most of them slope decisively. There are numerous doglegs and water hazards to navigate, too, and even on holes that seem straight, like the 346-yard eighth, it's easy to hit through the fairway if you don't put a gentle fade on your drive to hold it against the hill.

The seventh hole, a 399-yard par four, is a perfect example of the need for intelligent driving. The hole turns strongly right about 225 yards from the tee, with water just a few yards beyond the outside turn. A moderately-long driver of the ball will end up with a ball in the hazard unless he or she can fade it precisely off the tee. On the back, the 459-yard seventeenth hole, a par five, looks like it should be a birdie fest but a creek bisects the fairway at about 250 yards downhill, forcing most players to lay up off the tee and leaving a long, uphill second shot.

The back nine plays significantly longer than the front. At 3,270 yards (versus the front's 2,840), the incoming nine features a 530-yard uphill par five, a 400-yard water-carry par four, and the challenging 440-yard par four finishing hole.

Westchester county invested heavily in Sprain Lake in the past year, extending the fairway on the treacherous third hole, expanding tee boxes, rerouting and improving cart paths, and tweaking a couple of greens. Sprain Lake may be short, but its steep greens and tight fairways make it a fun test for the thinking golfer.

THE SAINT ANDREW'S CLUB
HASTINGS

A branch from the original Apple Tree

Astounding Facts (2013)

Here are a few historical facts about St. Andrew's Golf Club in Hastings that are guaranteed to astound your friends and golf trivia fanatics:

• St. Andrew's is the oldest continuously existing golf club in the United States, established on November 14, 1888.

• The first photograph of golf in America was taken at St. Andrew's in 1888. It features Harry Holbrook, A.P.W. Kinnan, J.B. Upham, and John Reid with caddies Warren and Frederic Holbrook at St. Andrew's.

• The first recorded mixed foursome in America was played at St. Andrew's. Mrs. John Reid, paired with J.B. Upham, defeated the team of Miss Carrie Law and John Reid on March 30, 1889.

• The first known American golf "clubhouse" with its rudimentary "nineteenth hole" (the famous apple tree) was established at St. Andrew's in 1892.

• St. Andrew's participated in the first inter-club team matches played in the US on October 9, 1894, along with Tuxedo (host), Brookline, and Shinnecock. St. Andrew's tied for first place with Brookline but couldn't stay another day for a play-off, since the first US Amateur/US Foursome/US Open tournaments started in two days' time at St. Andrew's.

• St. Andrew's was the host of the first US Amateur Championship, held under match-play format (as all the UK tournaments of the period were conducted), in 1894.* The first US Amateur Championship was won by a St. Andrew's member, L. B. Stoddart, in 1894.*

• St. Andrew's hosted the first US Open Championship, also in 1894.*

• St. Andrew's hosted the first US Foursome (two players per team playing alternate shots) Tournament. Held in conjunction with the above-mentioned US Amateur and US Open championships, this event was short-lived on the national scene.

• The team of L.B. Stoddart and J.B. Upham from St. Andrew's won the inaugural US Foursomes Tournament, 1894. They defeated another St. Andrew's pair, T.C. Ten Eyk and W.E. Hodgeman, in the all-St. Andrew's final.

• St. Andrew's member/official Henry O. Tallmadge suggested and organized the December 22, 1894, meeting of five golf clubs at the Calumet Club in NYC, which resulted in today's USGA.

• St. Andrew's published the first Club Yearbook (or Club Handbook) in the US containing a list of members, officers of the club, the various committees, and constitution and by-laws, in 1895.

• The first golf club in the US formed by women was the Saegkill Golf Club, organized by St. Andrew's women (Mrs. John Reid among them), in 1895.

• St. Andrew's organized and funded the first US Public Links Tournament at Van Courtlandt park (the first public course in the US), with a field of 50 golfers officiated by John Reid, in 1896. This tournament was "for players who did not belong to a club in the United States Golf Association."

*These championships are regarded by some as unofficial, as they were held prior to the formation of the USGA the following year. However, there is no dispute that they were the first amateur and open national golf championships ever held in the United States.

The First US Open? (2020)

On Oct. 4, 1895, the first official US Open Championship was conducted by the USGA on the nine-hole course of Newport (R.I.) Golf and Country Club. The USGA itself had been founded in December the year before and the Open was somewhat of an afterthought to the first US Amateur, also played that week on the same course. The winner was Horace Rawlins, 21, an English pro at the host course, who won $150 and a gold medal.

But there's a backstory to the US Open that begins at St. Andrew's in Hastings. The club had recently moved to Grey Oaks on the Saw Mill River, where it built a nine-hole course that hosted the first National Amateur Tournament in October of 1894, a few weeks before the founding of the USGA. L.B. Stoddard of the host club defeated Charles B. Macdonald of Chicago at the new St. Andrew's course.

That same week, St. Andrew's also hosted the first US Open—at least that's what it was called at the time. Four top professional golfers played a tournament of their own, competing for a first prize gold medal and $100. The winner was Willie Dunn, the pro at Shinnecock Hills, who also designed the original Ardsley Casino course (now Ardsley Country Club) and became its first club pro when it opened in 1896.

Largest Deal in Golf (2013)

Andrew Carnegie enjoyed golf so much, he built a home next to St. Andrew's in Hastings.

It's probably impossible to prove, but it's entirely likely that a deal spawned with him at the club may have been the largest ever struck on a golf course. I ran across this interesting tidbit in *American Colossus: The Triumph of Capitalism 1865-1900* by H.W. Brands. The club, which celebrated its 125th anniversary this year, played an essential role in the sale of member Andrew Carnegie's steel interests to J.P. Morgan and others in 1901.

The deal was a perfect example of the role golf can play in business—not to mention the value of scoring judiciously when playing against your boss.

Carnegie Steel President Charles M. Schwab was the hero of the piece. Morgan had made it known he and his partners wanted to buy out Carnegie so they could monopolize the steel industry. Schwab saw the value of the deal (he subsequently became president of the company it created, US

Steel) but the ultimate decision was Carnegie's, who wasn't particularly interested in selling. His wife, Louise, though, wanted him to retire. Here's how Brands described what happened:

"Louise Carnegie conspired with Schwab against her husband. Shortly after Schwab informed her of the merger scheme, she telephoned to say that Carnegie would be playing golf the next morning at St. Andrew's Club in Westchester. He was always more cooperative after winning at the Scottish national sport, she suggested. Schwab took the hint, whiffed a few for the cause, and broached the subject of selling. Carnegie didn't reject the plan outright, which Schwab took to be a good sign."

It was. The next morning, Carnegie named his price, $480 million. Morgan accepted it and a few days later closed the deal personally. As he shook Carnegie's hand, he said, "Mr. Carnegie, I want to congratulate you on being the richest man in the world."

At that point in time, it probably wasn't an exaggeration. The deal would be worth about $13 billion in today's dollars. That has to make it one of the biggest ever born on a golf course.

Notable Holes

St. Andrew's #4 (JF)

#4, 401 yards, par 4 - (2022) Few shots in golf are as soul-satisfying as a drive from an elevated tee that falls from the sky to a valley fairway far below. The fourth hole at St. Andrew's GC provides that wonderful experience as well as tremendous views of at least a half-dozen holes on the course from the tee. Beware the beast, though. He lurks behind the sharply-elevated and even more sharply-contoured green.

#9, 568 yards, par 5 - (2011) I wonder what John Reid and the "Apple Tree Gang" would think about this Jack Nicklaus design. It is probably longer than the total yardage of the three holes they played when the club was founded by the Scottish sportsman and his buddies in 1888 and I can guarantee it's harder. Those pioneering golfers established what became the oldest continuously operating golf club in the United States and one of the founding members of the USGA. Somehow, I think they would have been proud to play this long, difficult hole, although I doubt their gutta percha balls would make the carry from the back tee to the fairway, much less travel up the hill to the green in regulation. Today's players have to make sure they don't drive through the fairway off the tee, then stay out of the creek on the right side with their second shot. The third—and there will be a third shot on this monster uphill hole—is into a well-bunkered two-tiered green.

St. Andrew's #2 (JF)

#2, 325 yards, par 4 - (2020) Head pro Greg Bisconti immediately identified the second hole at St. Andrew's as a good hole that requires thought. "Although it's a short par 4 that is potentially reachable off the tee, you have to decide if it is worth the risk. There are penalty areas left and long and the closer you get to the green the trickier the pitch becomes. You'll have a downhill lie to an elevated green that has a swale in the left center ready to catch any shot that does not have the required spin to control the ball. The more prudent play is to hit a shot no more than 210 yards off the tee and leave yourself a full 90-110 yards into the green. Now you are able to hit a full shot and control the spin and thus the ball as it hits the green."

#8, 449 yards, par 4 - (2016) A solid drive in the fairway brings you to the real difficulty on the long "Road Hole" at St. Andrew's. Both distance and direction of your second shot have to be perfect to make par since the green can be a short game nightmare. There can be as much as a four-club difference in the distance for your approach since the green is a full 45 yards deep. It's a classic Biarritz with a false front, a middle canyon, and a back tier. If your ball lands on the wrong level, you'll have an interesting putt—or two or three. Just to keep you honest, the green is also rather narrow and four bunkers lurk along the right side.

#18, 421 yards, par 4 - (2017) Your approach to the green makes or breaks your score on the final hole (and most others) at St. Andrew's. It's an exciting finish, too, because there's no conservatively safe way to play it. The fairway is invitingly wide off the tee, but the green is elevated and pro-tected by deep, deep bunkers across the left front. When the cup is behind them, avoiding the bunkers by aiming to the right side will at best leave you with an impossible lag putt up and over the ridge that bisects the green front to back.

#10, 219 yards, par 3 - (2007) One of the most unusual hazards in Westchester is out of bounds on the tenth hole at St. Andrews, America's oldest continuously existing golf club, established in 1888 and moved to this property in 1897. The tenth hole is a new one, added ten years ago when Jack Nicklaus redesigned the venue. Like all OB's, this one is marked by white stakes. Many players don't even notice the stakes, however, be-cause they're dwarfed by a three-story granite cliff face right behind them that runs the entire length of the hole.

"It's a very dramatic hole," says head pro Charlie Hicks. "The whole right side is a huge rock outcropping. If you push it high enough and far enough right, it just stays there." Pushing it hard right is what happens, of course, when most players try to hit their tee shot a little harder, the natural inclination when faced with a 219-yard par three. It's entirely possible that your errant ball will carom off the monolith, too, but that shot is normally reserved for billiards.

The solution? Play it safely left. But watch out! As Hicks says, "The green drops off severely to the left. If you hook the ball at all, it ends up all the way down on the ninth fairway." Even if you put your tee shot on the immense putting surface, the green can be hazardous itself, with a swale as deep as the Mariana Trench running across it from side to side.

THE SUMMIT CLUB
ARMONK

Summit Club #8

(2021) The Summit Club at Armonk officially opened its full eighteen-hole golf course this week with a ribbon cutting ceremony on the first tee that marked a major milestone in a development that's been ten years in the making.

"It's very satisfying to be standing here after these last ten years, playing a golf course that we worked very hard on," says co-managing partner Jeff Mendell. "This is just the beginning. A couple of years down the road, the golf course will continue to be improved, both in terms of playability and esthetics. In the next phase, we will begin construction of 73 luxury condos, build a new clubhouse and sports pavilion, and create what I always envisioned for this property, a very special country club community here in Westchester."

The Summit Club began as Brynwood Golf and Country Club when Mendell and other partners bought the former Canyon Club from Mitsubishi a decade ago. Drawn out negotiations with the town of North Castle and some shuffling of ownership delayed the project and eventually closed the course. Mendell stuck with it, however, and revived the project last year along with a new co-managing partner, Chris Schiavone. The first step was getting the golf course into shape.

Members have been playing the front nine following upgrades to bunkers, tee boxes, and green complexes that was completed in the spring. The back nine took a few months longer as it underwent significant changes that included construction of three completely new holes and major renovation of two others, a renovation that significantly improved playability. The course is now 6,700 yards from the back tees with a par of 71.

"The way the course used to be on the back," explains Bryce Swanson, the Rees Jones design associate who managed the project, "was you had four par fours in a row on holes eleven through fourteen that were all similar in length and rather mediocre. We broke that up by making fourteen a dramatic risk-and-reward par five where you have to decide whether you want to challenge the creek 80 yards in front of the green by going for it in two. We also created a landing area for a layup that will give you a nice 100-yard wedge shot into the green.

"That hole flows nicely into a short par three, followed by two holes built from the old seventeenth hole. Sixteen is a risk-reward par four with a new green that brings the water into play. The new seventeen is a dramatic par three with a visually stunning drop shot." A couple of problematic fairways on the front nine were also reshaped and bunkers repositioned to better challenge modern golfers.

"We have a beautiful location here," says Schiavone. "with views and golf that any level of player can enjoy while still challenging you from the back tees if you want that. We're also going to make it an affordable club and gear events towards families. It will be more fun and less stiff than the usual club style. We're offering a club to a market that has a lot of great golf, but doesn't really serve that niche."

Notable Holes

#18, 477 yards, par 5 - (2012) It is possible to reach the green in two on the eighteenth hole at the Summit Club, but it takes a couple of mighty blows to do it. The hole plays not only uphill but sidehill most of the way, and the design of the green complex discourages a go-for-it second shot. It may be hard to believe that a 477-yard par five is a three-shot hole, but this one is.

Even then, it's not exactly an automatic par. The fairway is invitingly wide—except where you want to land your ball. It also tilts to the left, so drives that land in the center may well end their run in the rough. From the tee, you can aim at the bunker on the right side of the fairway, but be aware that it's about 250 yards away, so a good drive will find it. The bunker also serves another purpose—it makes the fairway only about fifteen yards wide at that point.

There's another bunker awaiting your second shot. This one's on the left side of the fairway about 100 yards from the green—exactly where you'd want to lay up. You can go ahead and bomb over it, just remember that you're still hitting uphill, so you'll need another club to clear the bunker. Three traps guard the green, two on the left and one on the right, but the toughest obstacle to par is the tree on the left front.

#8, 216 yards, par 3 - (2015) "For a bogey golfer, the most important thing stepping onto our eighth hole is to be on the right tee box," advises head pro Michael Mercadante. "A lot of golfers try to play from the back tee and so they have to hit driver—and hit it perfectly—just to get it there." On the scorecard, the hole doesn't look like it requires a driver. When you see the water and bunker in front of the steeply elevated green, though, you realize it takes a mighty blow to reach the putting surface. "Your best miss is to come up short," Mercadante says. "You don't want to miss left or right because you have a daunting chip to the undulating green. From the front, you can use a little backstop on the green. Short and right of the bunkers works for a lot of players. They then get on and have a putt for par or hopefully at worst a two-putt bogey."

#14, 530 yards, par 5 - (2020) Risk and reward is the theme on one of the newest holes in Westchester, the fourteenth at The Summit Club. In one of several major improvements to the old Brynwood CC course under the direction of architect Rees Jones, the club stretched a picturesque par four with ponds along the left side into a fun but challenging par five. Managing partner Jeff Mendel explains, "We took down the old elevated green to fairway level and built a new one a hundred yards or so farther away across the creek where the sixteenth tee used to be." The hole will measure about 530 yards, giving big hitters a chance to reach in two if they're willing to challenge the hole with an approach shot that needs to carry about 240 yards to clear the creek and a false front.

SUNNINGDALE GOLF CLUB
SCARSDALE

Sunningdale First Tee

Centennial Celebration (2013)

As Sunningdale Country Club marks its centennial this year, the members will be playing one of the most frequently updated courses in Westchester. For this year, new green complexes for the fourth and eighth holes were designed by architect Mike DeVries, who has been executing a long range plan for the club.

Actually, the founding members played their first three seasons on nine holes in Mount Vernon that had been vacated by Siwanoy Country Club. They moved to the current site in 1916, a piece of property with historic ties to the American Revolutionary War. In 1781, it served as an encampment for the French forces when they joined the Colonists in their fight for independence.

When the club moved, Seth Raynor was retained to lay out a new course on 149 acres containing The Overlook Golf Course, a private course owned by Thomas Simpson. The new track opened for play in 1918, but alterations began almost immediately for reasons lost to the ages. Walter Travis, noted amateur champion and designer of Westchester Country Club, was hired to build five new greens and several new tees and bunkers in 1920.

The renovated course apparently still didn't satisfy the members, so A.W. Tillinghast was brought in in 1929 to handle some re-routing and other changes, probably intended to eliminate some blind shots that had proven irksome to the membership.

Recent work has involved not so much restoration as redesign to take advantage of the gently rolling landscape and toughening up the contours of several greens that had become flatter with the passage of time. Several holes were lengthened and more than a few elephants were buried in some of the greens.

Notable Holes

#3, 215 yards, par 3 - (2006) Sunningdale is where the French forces encamped when they joined the American colonials in their fight against the British in 1781. This hole would make a good defensive position for anybody's army.

What you see from the tee is a wide, inviting green waiting for you on the other side of a picturesque valley where a line of apple trees leads down to a pond and the remnants of an old stone wall. But don't be fooled by the pastoral setting—the hole is long, long, long.

It plays even longer than it measures because the green is elevated higher than the tee, a fact you may not realize until you get on the green and look back. If you are deceived and hit your tee shot short of the green, it will roll forty yards back down the steep, closely-trimmed apron. If you navigate the three traps guarding either side of the green, you still have to deal with a swale running through the middle that divides the putting surface into two treacherous tiers.

#18, 475 yards, par 4 - (2017) Head pro Chris Toulson believes the new eighteenth hole at Sunningdale is the hardest finishing hole in Westchester—and he may well be right. "It's a doozie," he says. "You drive out of a chute of trees to a fairway that's slightly uphill and generally plays into the wind. There are two fairway bunkers strategically placed and a small, crowned green that's bunkered on the right side and behind. Left of the green is a tightly-mown chipping area." The entirely new hole is a fitting exclamation point to a multi-year course renovation by Mike DeVries completed this past winter.

#16, 560 yards, par 5 - (2023) Head pro Christopher Toulson says every shot counts on this long par 5. "The ideal tee shot is down the right-hand side of the fairway, but Underhill Road and out-of-bounds lurk right. If you drive conservatively to the left, your next shot becomes more challenging since it will be played into an area that is gradually narrowed by a creek on the right and a penalty area on the left. You can avoid this trouble by laying back, but then you will be faced with a third shot from a tricky down-hill lie. Because the green is small and elevated and usually firm, having a shorter third shot from a level lie increases your chances of holding the green. But in order to access this level area you'll have to play a bold second shot with a longer club. The sixteenth green is spectacular. It cants gently from left to right with a subtle spine running through its center. If you miss-hit your approach shot, the green's fierce false front will sweep your ball back, leaving you with an exacting uphill chip. The golfer will want a shorter approach into this demanding green, which in turn, puts a premium on a well-played drive and second shot."

TRUMP NATIONAL GOLF CLUB
BRIARCLIFF MANOR

Long before Donald Trump was President of the United States, one of his first ventures in golf was the course that became Trump Westchester. He acquired the financially-troubled Briar Hall Country Club in 1996, closed it in 1999 for significant renovations, and reopened in 2002 with a new golf course designed by Jim Fazio.

Notable Holes

#13, 218 yards, par 3 - (2007) Water seems to fall even from the sky on this, the most expensive if not the most hazardous hole in Westchester. The 101-foot waterfall thunders down behind the green, then races around to a shorter cataract in front and finally empties into the lake you have to carry from the tee.

It's spectacular, of course, but also distracting as hell, which may have been Jim Fazio's intent when he designed the hole. The Donald was just being his usual build-me-the-biggest, make-a-mark-on-the-world, can-you-top-this when he conceived it.

You would think the water would be enough, but your tee shot also has to rocket through a narrow chute of trees that line the flight path to the green. Playing this hole in the wind is like trying to land an F-16 during a gale on the flight deck of the USS Enterprise.

#2, 515 yard, par 5 - (2026) Memories come early in the round at Trump National in Briarcliff Manor, and not all of them are pleasant. The second hole has so many ways to go wrong that one member (who prefers anonymity) once scored a 22, earning him the moniker of "Double Deuce" from his hard-ribbing friends. Out of bounds to the right, water that must be carried off the tee, then Barron's Creek very much in play the entire length of the hole can quickly put double digits on your scorecard.

WACCABUC COUNTRY CLUB
WACCABUC

Waccabuc Country Club was organized in 1912 by a group of local residents to play the nine-hole course on the grounds of the Lake Waccabuc Inn, a genteel country resort. In 1927, the club took over the property and the inn became its club-house. In 1923, the course was expanded to 18 holes that were basically designed by the members with the assistance of the club pro, Jack Bullen. The club brought in Alfred Tull in 1962 to give it a complete overhaul.

A marker on the lawn in front of the clubhouse states that the distance to New York City is 52 miles. The stone dates to the Colonial era and was part of a system designed by Benjamin Franklin when he was Postmaster of the United States.

Notable Holes

#13, 466 yards, par 4 - (2012) Head pro John McPhee plays this long, straight hole with a driver and a hybrid, but then he also holds the course record of 62 and obviously knows what he's doing. In truth, as long as you can hit it straight, there's no reason not to score well here. A line of trees presents the biggest problem to those who stray off the fairway left and there are more to the right, although there's a little more room on that side. You're going to have a long approach shot no matter where you are, though, so it's essential you make it from the short grass.

The green is deep—over thirty yards—so club selection for the second shot is not automatic. Running the ball onto the green isn't unusual since it is level in the front. The back half slopes sharply back to front, though, so read your putts carefully if the pin is anywhere behind the mid-point.

#9, 197 yards, par 3 - (2014) "This is a very difficult, very long par three," says head pro Martin Granda. "Every shot has to be good. If you miss the green from the tee, you have to be short because it's a hard up-and-down from anywhere besides the fairway. The green has a lot of movement on it, too—more than you think!"

WESTCHESTER COUNTRY CLUB
RYE

Westchester Country Club West #1

The Epitome of the Good Life (2022)

Westchester Country Club is recognized internationally as a PGA and LPGA Tour stop and has hosted two national USGA championships, but it's best known locally as the epitome of the good life in Westchester County.

How large is the good life at Westchester Country Club? Its 1,500 members and their families and guests enjoy three golf courses, a world-class golf practice facility, an eight-story clubhouse with 400 rooms, every paddle sport known to man, and not just a swimming pool but an entire 62-acre beach club with 1,000 feet of sand beach on Long Island Sound. It's easily the largest country club in the county.

As NBC Golf broadcaster Jimmy Roberts says, "It's grand. They just don't make places like this anymore." The Rye resident is a long-time member of WCC and adds, "There's an intimacy about it, despite the size. It's a club where you can get close to people." Roberts, a 13-time Emmy Award winner, believes the golf courses are among the finest he's seen. "The West

Course has true character, perhaps the eighteen best green complexes you'll find on tour."

Bowman's vision

A hundred years ago, hotelier John Bowman had a vision. The president of Biltmore Hotels hoped to cap a stellar career by building a planned community for millionaire sportsmen on 583 acres of land in Harrison purchased from the Hobart Park estate. He added several other parcels, including 62 acres on nearby Manursing Island in Rye. When it opened in 1922, the community had everything a Golden Age sportsman could want including golf courses, polo grounds, tennis, stables, boating, swimming, and shooting, as well as a luxurious hotel with both private apartments and guest rooms and grounds for private homes that would be serviced by the hotel's staff.

Money was no object to Bowman, but lack of it proved to be his downfall. By 1929, he had spent well over $6 million to build the facilities (three times his initial $2 million budget) and was more than $5 million in the red, jeopardizing the health of the parent hotel corporation. The members of the club banded together and bought the properties for $5.8 million to preserve their interests and insure their big slice of heaven would survive.

Golf remains the centerpiece of the club, with two world-class eighteen-hole courses, a nine-hole par three course, and one of the most complete practice and learning facilities anywhere. When John Bowman built the courses, he hired Walter Travis, one of the leading architects of the day as well as a stellar player who won major tournaments including the US Amateur three times. Travis was the first American to win the British Amateur.

The West Course is known as a challenge for even the best players in the game, but it's original design was a real monster. When it opened, the course played to par 76 at 6,733 yards, which was a long, long golf course in 1921 when steel shafted golf clubs were novelties. It also had over 100 bunkers, including many cross bunkers that pestered short hitters, which included just about everybody. Today, following extensive renovations by the Fazio Group, the course measures 6,718 yards, par 72, but has forty fewer bunkers.

Travis intended the South Course to be less difficult so everyday golfers would have a course to play that wouldn't break their spirits every time they teed it up. The South retains that purpose today but can be quite challenging in its own right. From the tips, the course plays 6,623 yards, nearly as long as the West, with par of 71.

"One unusual feature that Westchester has is two completely different, both very good, golf courses," according to Director of Golf Ben Hoffhine. "The West Course is hard enough to challenge the best players in the world.

The South Course is a challenge from the back tees but is very user friendly for the shorter-hitting player. The course designs indicate how inclusive the club was meant to be."

Hoffhine points out that when the club was founded, it had full, bond-holding women members. Today, he says, "Our ladies associations have 300 members and 50% of our junior players are girls." With an eye toward the future, Hoffhine says the club has placed particular emphasis on young golfers. "The goal of our junior program is to expose children to the game so they fall in love with it. "We have over 100 kids involved in junior golf," he says. "We're starting a program for three-year-olds this year."

Opening Day

On May 15, 1922, opening day for Westchester Biltmore Country Club was marked by an exhibition match played by the reigning 1921 PGA Champion, Walter Hagen, teamed with "Long Jim" Barnes, who held the 1921 US Open title, earned while serving as head pro at newly-opened Pelham CC. They took on WCC's first head professional, Cuthbert Butchart, and then-amateur Tommy Armour. The "locals" beat the national headline makers 2-up.

That same year, the club hosted the concluding half of the "Golf Championship of the World" in October. The 72-hole contest between Walter Hagen and Gene Sarazen had begun the day before at Oakmont CC in Pittsburgh, with the two boarding an overnight train for New York to finish the match in Westchester. The pair were inarguably the leading golfers of the day. Hagen was a four-time major winner at that point in his career including the 1922 British Open. Local hero Sarazen, who was born in Harrison and caddied at the Apawamis Club next door, had won both the US Open and the PGA Championship that year. Sarazen came from behind to top Hagen 3-2 in the 36-hole final, collected his $2,000 prize check, then went to St. Luke's Hospital in Yonkers for an emergency appendectomy.

WCC hosted its first national golf championship in 1923 and its second in 2021. Both were the USGA's US Women's Amateur. Underdog Edith Cummings won the 1923 event the week before the Yankees and Giants were to meet in the World Series. Last year, another underdog, Jensen Castle, battled through 36 holes of medal play, three rounds of single-elimination stroke play, and a 36-hole stroke-play final match to take home the Robert Cox Cup.

Years with the PGA Tour

The PGA Tour made Westchester its home for nearly 50 years, beginning with the 1963 Thunderbird Classic, won by Arnold Palmer, and ending with the Senior Players Championship in 2011, where Fred Couples took home the first place trophy. The club is best known, however, as the venue for the Westchester Classic, which began in 1967 with a win by Jack Nicklaus. It came to an end following an ugly dispute between the club and the PGA Tour when the FedEx Cup was inaugurated by the playing of The Barclays in 2007. Steve Stricker won that event, joining a gallery of Classic winners that included nearly every outstanding player in the game. Vijay Singh won three times, Nicklaus, Sergio Garcia, Ernie Els, and Seve Ballesteros won it twice.

Some highlights of the Classic over the years included a double eagle by Bob Guilder on the closing hole of his third round in 1982. Only the spectators saw the 251-yard three wood, however, since CBS had paused for a commercial break just before he hit it. A plaque marks the spot in the fairway of the ninth hole (as members play the course).

Ben Hogan, 58 years old, played his final competitive round at the Classic on July 30, 1970, carding a 78 and withdrawing from the tournament.

JC Snead, nephew of Sam Snead and one-time assistant pro at Century CC in Purchase, defeated Seve Ballesteros in a one-hole playoff in 1987. The aggressive Spaniard tried to drive the green on the short first hole (as played by the members), but pulled his shot into an impossible position. Snead calmly played a four iron from the tee to the middle of the fairway, pitched on, and won the tournament.

The most recent professional championship to be played at WCC was the 2015 KPMG Women's PGA Championship, a major formerly known as the LPGA Championship. Inbee Park became only the second player to win the tournament three times in succession, tying Annika Sorenstam.

Westchester CC President Mark Christiana says, "The future of WCC is very bright. We continue to make investments in all areas of our facilities to meet the needs of current and future members."

The success of the KMPG and the US Women's Amateur drew the attention of the sport's governing bodies. It wouldn't be surprising to see Westchester Country Club host more world-class events in the near future.

US Women's Amateur Championship (2021)

The West Course at Westchester Country Club hosts one of the longest, hardest tournaments in women's golf next week. It's the 121st US Women's Amateur Championship and it stretches from two rounds of medal play on Monday and Tuesday through six rounds of match play concluding with a 36-hole final on Sunday.

Playing at 6,488 yards and par 72, the course will provide a sturdy test for the women with its undulating terrain and strongly-contoured greens. The players will face firm, fast, narrow fairways protected by lush, three-inch primary rough, not to mention deep fescue and rocky outcroppings.

"You have to be accurate with your drives because the rough is super penal," says reigning US Women's Mid-Amateur Champion Ina Kim-Schaad, who will be in the field. "The greens, even though they are large, are very firm and very fast. You can't even be pin-high. You have to stay below the hole to have a chance. It's a real shot-maker's course. You need a good short game, too, because if you miss the green, it's really hard to get up and down."

The West Course was a PGA Tour stop for over 40 years. Winners include Arnold Palmer, Jack Nicklaus, Seve Ballesteros, Johnny Miller, Ernie Els, Vijay Singh, and Padraig Harrington. Most recently, it hosted the KPMG Women's PGA Championship, won by Inbee Park.

The field of 156 players is made up of the best women amateur golfers from around the world as well as close to Westchester. In addition to Kim-Schaad, who is from Rhinebeck, N.Y., players include Megha Ganne, of Holmdel, N.J., who was the low amateur in the 2021 US Women's Open, Kelly Sim, of Edgewater, N.J., Angelina Tolentino, Mount Laurel, N.J., and Lauren Peter, Carmel, N.Y.

Ganne says she has played the course once and expects it to be quite a challenge. "Ball striking, putting, and course management have to be perfect. There are a lot of birdie-able holes but you can make a nine on them real quick, too."

As usual, the nines will be reversed for the championship, which will heighten the excitement of the match play format. Director of Golf Ben Hoffine says "The finishing holes will be very interesting. Fifteen is a very difficult par four, sixteen is a difficult par three, then you have two birdie holes to finish in seventeen and eighteen. If matches come down to the last two, you'll see some fireworks."

The USGA will use a lot of different tees and hole locations. It's expected that the tenth hole will be drive-able for longer hitters and the twelfth is a very reachable par five from a carefully placed tee shot. Hoffhine points out that players will have a decision to make on hole fifteen, a long par four with a dogleg right protected by a large tree. "Even with a good drive, the second shot will require a hybrid or long iron. It's a blind shot, too, and the green is one of the most difficult on the course."

The championship was first played in 1895. It was held at Westchester CC in 1923, and was won by Edith Cummings. Notable champions from the tournament history include Lydia Ko, Morgan Pressel, Juli Inkster, Babe Didrickson Zaharias, and Patty Berg.

KPMG Women's PGA Championship (2015)

Westchester CC West #3

Westchester Country Club drew rave reviews Monday as the PGA of America and LPGA began ramping up preparations for the KPMG Women's PGA Championship to be played on the club's West Course June 11-14. The comments came as luminaries of the event addressed media to kick off the tournament buildup.

PGA of America CEO Pete Bevacqua said, "Having grown up in this area, when you talk about the quality of golf courses in the Met Section, you can't go five miles without bumping into one of the best golf courses in the country—but Westchester Country Club is special. Look at the championship pedigree of this golf course! I think back to coming here and watching the greatest players in the world. I remember shaking Seve Ballesteros's hand right outside this room when I was about eleven years old." He added another important reason: "They wanted to host the event. They wanted to be a part of this. I don't think you could pick a better venue for this event than Westchester Country Club."

Westchester CC hosted the PGA Tour from 1963 to 2007 and the Senior Players Championship in 2011. Grandstands, broadcast booths, concession tents and all the other infrastructure of a major golf tournament started going up this week for the club's first major tournament.

Also praising the course was Stacy Lewis, two-time major winner and spokesperson for tournament sponsor KPMG. "It definitely looks to me like a shot maker's golf course," she said. "You're going to have to hit shots to keep it in the fairways, hit into certain spots on greens. I think it's going to be a great test. It's going to be a long walk, I know that. But it's going to be a really good test of golf. As a major, it should be, but I think the rough and hitting fairways is going to be at a premium."

Lewis said she has been consulting with KPMG as they developed their relationship with golf and has been very pleased at their response to her suggestions. "KPMG asked me what we needed and I said we needed a big venue, a big purse and network TV. Those are kind of the three big things that I thought if we could get to all of our majors, really, eventually, that would really put us on the map. The big thing with this tournament I was most excited about was the venue."

Jean Bartholomew, four-time LPGA Teaching & Club Professional National Champion, remembered growing up on Long Island and playing junior events at the club. For the LPGA today, she said, "I always felt like we deserved to play on courses like this. And we do play on them; we are not putting down other tournaments. But coming to Westchester Country Club and seeing it and this whole event just has an air to it. There's a feel to it that it's just going to be beyond first class."

Bartholomew had some advice for golfers playing the course for the first time: "You have to manage your way, you're going to have to work your ball into some of the pins, and I think it's going to be difficult if you miss greens to get up and down because the greens are so undulating. It's going to be a great test."

Also speaking at the kick-off event were Mike Whan, LPGA Tour Commissioner, John Veihmeyer, KPMG Global Chairman, Dalynn Hoch, CFO, Zurich North America, Zurich Insurance Company, and Inbee Park, winner of the championship in 2013 and 2014.

Notable Holes

#2 West, 447 yards, par 4 - (2006) The second hole on the West Course, played as the eleventh during the tournament, starts with a drive downhill to a deceptively wide landing area that ends with a stone-lined creek that crosses the fairway 300 yards out. What should you think of when you stand on the tee? Member John Peterson advises, "Ball placement." Even after a perfect drive, a long approach shot remains to a very tight, three-tiered green, which breaks from left to right.

The green is guarded by an immense elm (not to mention three serious bunkers) that will block a second shot from anywhere except the left half of the fairway. Horse chestnut, sycamore, elm, sugar maples, and alder are part of the forest behind the green.

Westchester CC West #6 (JF)

#6 West, 430 yards, par 4 - (2015) Westchester Country Club Director of Golf John Kennedy points out that the sixth hole on the West course tests every golfer with two long shots to one of the most difficult greens of the eighteen. The hole is a long dogleg right, which means choosing the right set of tees is crucial for the bogey golfer so he or she can reach the crook in the dogleg. "Even if you get it past the trees on the right," Kennedy says, "you'll have a long, long, second shot up and over a hill. It's not a bad idea to play to the landing area in front of the green rather than try to reach it in regulation since the throat between the bunkers guarding the left and right side of the green is only eleven yards wide and misses are expensive."

#1 West, 314 yards, par 4 - (2008) A good risk and reward hole can break your heart or award you a trophy. The first hole at Westchester Country Club has done both many times. At 314 yards, it's drive-able if you dare. It's also eminently miss-able, as Seve Ballesteros found when he tried to reach it during a playoff with JC Snead for the Westchester Classic Championship in 1987. The gallant Spaniard went for broke, but a little too much right hand, a slight restriction in his turn, maybe a flighty right elbow, something sent his drive sailing down the hill left of the green, the last place you want to be on this hole. Snead watched Ballesteros take the risk and miss, then put his own driver back in the bag, laid up, pitched on, and won the tournament.

Westchester CC West #17 (JF)

#17 West, 435 yards, par 4 - (2021) The penultimate hole on the West Course at Westchester Country Club has always been one of the most interesting challenges on the course. The recent Tom Fazio re-do made it even better, according to assistant pro Dirk Giannotti, who says, "You now have more options, more sight lines, and more chances to make par." A massive rock outcropping on the corner of the tricky dogleg left was blasted into submission to provide another strategic option off the tee. The fairway was expanded to make more room for error, although water is still very much in play for long hitters who mistakenly drive their ball through the fairway. An entirely new angle of approach was opened up by removal of the tree that stood to the left of the green, one of the best changes on the course.

Westchester CC West #10 (JF)

#10 West, 180 yards, par 3 - Number ten looks so simple, but it's so, so hard. Teaching pro Sarah Stone says, "It's a great par three. You're going to be using a longer club like a mid-iron or a hybrid. There's out of bounds on the right and bunkers on either side so you have to hit your favorite club like a laser to the middle of the green. You can't really go at any pin, either, because the green structure is very challenging. Your ball can roll off the green left or right and long is death in the run-off collection area in the back. I often encourage players to take one less club and plan to putt from off the green."

#14 West, 575 yards, par 5 - (2012) Can you make this green in two? It's possible, but not probable. The hole plays downhill, so you will get a little extra from your drive if you put it in exactly the right place. The green is long and slightly elevated, though, so it's not likely anything but two big, big hits will get you there.

On the tee, take aim at the fairway bunker you see in the distance. That's a little over 300 yards from where you're standing, so you don't really have to worry about landing in it unless your name is Fred Couples. The most important thing to do off the tee is to hit a long, solid draw. You can cut the corner left, but if you over-pull just a little, the trees will get you.

Smart players decide how far they want to hit their third shot before they hit their second. The green has a false front you don't really see from the fairway, so make sure your approach carries all the way.

#3 West, 485 yards, par 5 - (2023) This hole offers a multitude of challenges and opportunities. It's a short par five, but the scorecard doesn't begin to tell the real story. "Off the tee," Director of Golf Ben Hoffhine explains, "the fairway is generous but flanked by bunkers. About 230 yards from the green the fairway pitches downhill, which can give your drive a big kick. Regardless of whether you get that advantage or not, you then have a decision to make. The green and approach are perched on top of a hill that's covered in thick rough from 90 yards in. Short is not good, so think twice before swinging for the fences. A lay-up to the 100 yard marker is safe, but it leaves a third shot severely up hill to a blind green. Once on the green, you have to navigate a ridge that plays havoc with many putts." After you hole your putt, Hoffhine says, "Look back down the fairway and over to the fourth hole, one of many great vistas on the golf course."

#9 South, 398 yards, par 4 - (2022) Beasts seen and unseen threaten the golfer who can't find the fairway from the tee on this hole. Unseen is the water left of the landing area, which comes into play on a long, erratic draw. Seen to the right, though, is a visually-stunning red barn that reflects the history of the property as a farm before it was purchased by John Bowman in 1919. Yes, the barn comes into play on the second shot from the rough for slicers off the tee.

#3 South, 492 yards, par 5 - (2025) This long, fun hole makes you think twice about the strategy for your second shot. The green sits at the bottom of a steep curve in the fairway, so if you dare, you can aim for the top and hope your ball runs down onto the green for an eagle try. The green's pretty small, though, so it may pay to settle for reaching it in regulation.

WESTCHESTER HILLS GOLF CLUB
WHITE PLAINS

Westchester Hills #8

Centennial Celebration (2013)

Westchester Hills celebrated its 100th Anniversary in 2013 with a Gatsby-themed Gala. Both Westchester County Executive Rob Astorino and White Plains Mayor Thomas Roach were on hand to offer congratulations and to present the Club with proclamations announcing September 28, 2013, as Westchester Hills Day in the County and in White Plains.

More than 220 members attended the celebration at the Club which included a cocktail hour on the first tee and a celebratory dinner dance which continued into the early morning hours. Club President Mike Daly, a White Plains resident, delivered brief remarks congratulating various committees responsible for organizing the Centennial Gala before introducing the County Executive and the Mayor.

Westchester Hills was established in 1913 by Robert E. Farley who was the developer of Gedney Farms and the Gedney Farm Hotel. The construction of the Golf Course was supervised by Peter Clark, a Scot, who became the Club's first golf professional. The first 9 holes were completed in October 1913, the final 18 holes in July 1915.

Recently, a member-funded major reconstruction of the Clubhouse, patio and entrance way was completed resulting in an increase of membership and an increase in participation in Club activities. The Clubhouse was renovated from floor to ceiling revealing a fireplace, which had been covered over years ago, and vaulted ceilings which had also been covered. The Patio was expanded and an outdoor service area was added.

New and Old Design (2019)

Creative design and near-continuous change of its playing field separates golf from every other sport. Nowhere is that more evident than at Westchester Hills, where the golf course has continually evolved to match the ever-changing nature of the game. The club recently completed a multi-year course overhaul and erected a plaque this past winter recognizing the contributions of member Mark Stagg to the latest changes.

The more recent alterations enhanced a series of four holes on the back nine known as "The Horseshoe." While all four were substantially improved, some of the most apparent changes were on the downhill fifteenth hole where trees were removed along the fairway and a rock outcropping was moved away from the green. This also allowed a major change in the par three sixteenth hole, where the tee box now provides tremendous flexibility in setting up the hole's challenge.

This is far from the first major remodeling of Westchester Hills. The original design for the course, which opened in 1913, is credited to the club's first head pro, Peter Clark, with some assistance from Donald Ross. Less than ten years later, Walter Travis, the architect who created the two fine golf courses at Westchester Country Club, had a hand in the design of Westchester Hills, too. According to club records that Brian Giordano and Ed Homsey of the Travis Society found, Travis prepared plans for significant alterations to the course that were put into place in 1922. Giordano is the new head pro at Westchester Hills, the club's fifth in its 106-year history.

Rees Jones Renovation (2021)

Work to upgrade the golf experience continues at Westchester Hills. The club finished major drainage work on the greens over the winter and plans to install a new irrigation system this fall as part of a master plan developed by Rees Jones. As club president Joe Oates explains, "By moving the irrigation project to the fall of this year, we can complete the Rees Jones redesign work at the same time and reduce the disruption to our membership from two separate large golf course projects."

The redesign work will touch nearly every hole on the course and focus on the scoring areas of the game, the greens and surrounds. "We're going to restore the sizes to give the greens more pin positions," Jones explains. "We'll also renovate the bunkers to a pre-Depression style, using modern technology."

Over time, greens tend to become smaller, the contours change somewhat, and their playing characteristics are altered as a result of normal mowing and other maintenance. The restorations will not only bring most of the greens back to their original sizes but will also result in new playing strategies for some, including the difficult fourteenth hole, an uphill par three. In addition, many of the green surrounds will incorporate tightly-mowed chipping areas to give players more options.

Notable Holes

#6, 529 yards, par 5 - (2008) How much faith do you have in your three wood? A solid drive anywhere in the fairway on this classic risk and reward par five gives you the chance to demonstrate that faith by bombing your second shot over the water and onto the green. "You have to flirt with the water to get your reward," according to head pro Jason Gobleck. Just make sure you hit it straight as well as long, because fescue rough lines the entire left side of the hole and a creek runs along the right. There is a miniscule bail-out area just to the right of the green, but it's almost easier to hit the green itself.

#9, 303 yards, par 4 - (2010) Just for a change of pace from long and mean, how about a hole that's short and mean? The ninth hole at Westchester Hills fits that bill perfectly. At only 303 yards, it dares you to pull the driver out of the bag and smash one straight away toward the green that sits so tantalizingly close. The landing area is a little tight, of course, but why worry about a few trees when you can almost will your ball to land in the fairway? And that big bunker stretching across the entire front of the green? Ignore it—your ball will probably stop right in front of it leaving a simple little pitch to the strongly sloped green. Before you take the cover off your driver, though, check the tee markers. The bunker is 260 yards from the back but only 230 from the front of the tee box. And those trees? They are a mere 19 yards apart in the landing area.

#7, 344 yards, par 4 - (2012) The seventh at Westchester Hills is a nasty little hole fully capable of bringing tears to the eyes of grown men—especially those who think they have the game to overpower it. Like most short par fours, the best way to play this hole is with your brain, not your brawn.

You are welcome to pound a driver off the tee as long as you can hit it laser straight. That picturesque wooden fence you see running the length of the hole on the right is out of bounds. Notice how close it is to the fairway? Maybe it's a sign you should be using a scalpel instead of a chainsaw to dissect this hole.

Even if you play it safe, however, there's no assurance that your second shot will nestle up close to the pin. The green is the size of a ping pong table and just about as hard to hold with anything other than a perfect floating wedge. Complicating matters are three bunkers, one of which—the deepest, naturally—is inconveniently located right in front of the green.

THE WHIPPOORWILL CLUB
ARMONK

Whippoorwill #13 (JF)

Fans of golf architect Charles Banks—myself among them—rank Whippoorwill as one of his masterpieces. The course rises and falls over stunning topography that perfectly fits "Steamshovel" Banks's giant undulating greens and canyon-size bunkers.

Banks wasn't the first architect to build a course for the club, however. Donald Ross constructed a nine-hole course that opened in 1927. The members (and the first head pro, Fred Ruth), soon decided they wanted something more and retained Banks to design today's 18 holes. The club ran headlong into financial troubles during the Great Depression and operated as a semi-private club, then ceased operations entirely until 1942. It was saved by Louis Calder, who paid off the club's debt and incorporated today's Whippoorwill Club in 1946.

Notable Holes

#7, 423 yards, par 4 - (2007) This treacherous dogleg par four plays much longer than its yardage, both mentally and physically. The tee shot is interesting, to say the least. It's a forced carry over a pond and then around a large mound in the fairway. Local legend has it that a steam shovel was lost in the pond during construction of the course in 1928. If so, it's covered by wet golf balls today.

The fairway begins 175 yards off the tee; a straight 200 yard drive gives you an off-balance lie on a grassy mound and 280 puts you through the fairway and out of the hole. The perfect tee shot is a well-controlled draw, which will leave you a couple hundred yards from the green. Head Pro Jim Wahl advises, "You can try to cut a little off the corner by hitting a fairway wood or hybrid, but those trees will catch you."

Once you get around the dogleg, the uphill second shot is hazardous, too. It plays two clubs longer than its distance, which makes it hard to thread the needle to a green protected by a sharp false front and two big mounds on either side. The green is wide but only twenty yards deep, further complicating the approach. It sits in a bowl surrounded by grassy knolls that will either kick your ball onto the putting surface or swallow it whole.

#8, 196 yards, par 3 - (2010) Playing the eighth hole at Whippoorwill is like traveling to an exotic land. From the elevated tee you have an intimidating view of bunkers like desert wastelands that flank the green. Travel a little closer and you'll see the charming waterfall feeding the picturesque pond behind it. The Biarritz green itself is extraordinary. At 66 yards from front to back, it may be one of the longest in the county while its 16-yard width makes it one of the narrowest. Depending on the tee and pin positions, the hole can play from 139 to 229 yards. The most striking feature of all, though, is the knee-deep valley that splits the green into two parts—not something you want to putt through. Distance control, in other words, is the foreign language you need to learn to visit this exotic hole.

#18, par 4, 437 yards - (2022) The beast comes out on the tee shot on this harder-than-it-looks par four. A drive to the left, even if it's in the fairway, may not leave a manageable approach angle to the uphill green. Yet a fairway bunker on the right menaces the slicer. From the center of the fairway, it's worth a moment to enjoy not just your triumph, but the view of the modern classic clubhouse and the flags flying behind the green.

WINGED FOOT GOLF CLUB
MAMARONECK

Leo the Lion guards the Winged Foot clubhouse

A Winged Foot Century (2023)

Winged Foot Golf Club may be located in Mamaroneck, but it belongs to the world. Its two golf courses are perennially ranked among the best in the game, the club has hosted a long list of major tournaments, and its membership roster includes leaders in commerce, industry, media, medicine, and public service. As head professional Mike Gilmore says, "The whole world watches what Winged Foot does. It has tremendous stature in the golf world."

In 1921, a group of NY Athletic Club members lost a vote to build a golf course for the organization. Instead of filing lawsuits or storming the club's headquarters, the men incorporated Winged Foot Golf Club on their own, bought a 280-acre farm in Mamaroneck, and commissioned A.W. Tillinghast to build them a "man-sized course." Tilly built two and the first round was played on them in June of 1923.

Tillinghast reportedly moved 7,200 tons of rock to build the courses. Much of it can be found today in the classic English Scholastic-style clubhouse designed by Clifford Wendehack, where you'll also see a fascinating gallery of photos and memorabilia highlighting the club's storied history. "The quality of the golf courses and our investment in them is a statement that Winged Foot is here to stay," says recently-retired general manager Colin Burns. He backs up that statement by pointing to $70 million the club spent in recent years to upgrade not only the two golf courses but also employee housing, swim facilities, locker rooms, kitchens, and more.

Looking at the black wrought iron security gates, the imposing clubhouse, and the impeccable golf courses, you might think Winged Foot is a stiff and formal place. What most non-members don't know, though, is just how relaxed and friendly the club really is. "Winged Foot is a club first," says president Rob Williams, who joined as a junior member in 1986. " It happens to have an international reputation, but when people come here, they get to know each other; they're friends. Most of the members come from five or six towns around here. When you step into the Grill Room, you see that, whether you're a member or a guest."

Caddie manager and course starter David Zona has discretely observed the club members closeup for nineteen years. He says, "It's hallowed ground, but the membership is very welcoming, friendly, and down-to-earth. The bar opens early. They are here to play golf and have a good time. It's not a stuffy club, for sure."

Winged Foot kicked off its centennial celebration this year with the announcement that the club will host its seventh US Open in 2028. A three-day party over the opening Memorial Day weekend and a member-guest tournament in October featuring a long list of club professionals who once worked at the club will bookend numerous other anniversary-year observances. The club also established the Winged Foot Foundation this year to formalize the membership's long but ad-hoc tradition of supporting charitable causes. In addition, a centennial garden is under construction next to the clubhouse. The centerpiece will be a statue of the club's famous winged foot logo mounted on a pedestal along with displays recognizing the members of a newly-established Winged Foot Hall of Fame.

Among the inductees into the hall is Claude Harmon, one of several noted golf professionals who served as head pros for the club. Harmon won the 1948 Masters while working as head pro from 1945 to 1978. He was preceded by Craig Wood, who won both the US Open and the Masters in 1941 during his tenure at Winged Foot from 1939 to 1945. Tom Nieporte had won the Bob Hope Desert Classic before he succeeded Harmon in 1978, making him one of the last pros to succeed both on the PGA Tour and at the club level.

Two challenging courses

If there was a golf course hall of fame, both eighteen-hole tracks at Winged Foot would be charter members. Williams says, "What makes WFGC click is that the 36 holes that Tillinghast created are still stimulate players. You're not going to lose any golf balls, but you're going to be challenged by the design just as you would have been 100 years ago."

Both courses, the East at 6,808 yards and the West at 6,947 (7,426 yards for the US Open!) have hosted major tournaments and are among the world's finest examples of strategic design. Tillinghast said of his concept, "The contouring of the greens places a premium on the placement of the drives…. It is only the knowledge that the next shot must be played with rifle accuracy that brings the realization that the drive must be placed."

Then there are the greens, which even after the renovation and their expansion conducted by architect Gil Hanse, are small and treacherously contoured. Some of them drop as much as seven feet from back to front. Head pro Mike Gilmore cites the par three thirteenth hole on the East course as a prime example. "I call the green 'Armageddon'," he says. "I was nine under after ten on the East course one time, then I got to thirteen and finished five under."

The West Course is the better known of the two by virtue of its service as a US Open venue. The East, though, has hosted its own share of major tournaments. Gilmore points out, "The green complexes on the East are more difficult but the West is a longer course by a few yards. The East requires a variety of shots off the tee and makes you stop and think before you hit your approach shot. If you poll the members, a slim majority likes the East better than the West."

There are fabulous holes on both courses. Tillinghast reportedly considered ten West, with its sloping three-lobbed green protected by canyon-deep bunkers, the finest par three in the country. Ben Hogan, playing in the 1959 US Open and referring to the private home that sits behind the green, said the shot from the tee was a "three-iron into someone's bedroom." The dogleg on the par four eighteenth West crushed Phil Mickelson's dream of a US Open title in 2006 while the severe green on that same hole was the site of a miraculous putt by Bobby Jones to open the door to his US Open win in 1929.

Then there's the first hole on the West course, which is famous for another reason. That's where, according to legend, Winged Foot member David Mulligan often sprayed his tee shot in the nether regions away from the fairway. When his friends gave him a second chance, the shot became a "mulligan."

Winged Foot is known internationally as a US Open venue, but locally, it's the site of many other important events. The Anderson Memorial, named after club member John Anderson who won both the US and the British Amateurs, is the premier four-ball invitational tournament in the country. The club has also hosted the Met Open seven times, including the 100th anniversary of the tournament in 2015, and the Ike and the Met Amateur three times.

While Winged Foot celebrates its past hundred years, the club is already thinking about its next century. "We're marking the centennial with a big focus on what's to come," says club president Rob Williams. "We are here to stay and part of what we have to ask ourselves as stewards of the club is 'What are we going to do to be sure we stay relevant to the game?'" The world is watching to see what they decide.

US Open at Winged Foot

1929 - The first US Open held at Winged Foot GC was won by Bobby Jones in a playoff. Jones took the lead in the first round with a 69 and followed it with a 75 in the second. After a third round 71, he held a three-stroke lead over Harrison native Gene Sarazen. Sarazen faded in the final round and so did Jones, who triple-bogeyed the fifteenth hole and bogeyed the sixteenth to open the door for Al Espinosa. Jones threw the tournament into a playoff when he blasted out of a greenside bunker on 18 and sank an impossible 12-foot putt to tie Espinosa. He won handily by 23 strokes in a 36-hole playoff the following day to claim the title.

Head pro Mike Gilmore replicates the decisive Bobby Jones putt on #18 (JF)

It was the third time Jones had won the championship. He claimed his first US Open title at Inwood CC on Long Island in 1923, the year Winged Foot opened for play. He won that one in a playoff, too, over Bobby Cruikshanks, who later became head pro at Progress Country Club (the original name of Old Oaks CC), and the second in 1926 at Scioto CC in Ohio, where he defeated Joe Turnesa, one of Westchester's first family of golf.

1959 - Billy Casper's phenomenal putting clinched the title for him at the 1959 US Open at Winged Foot GC. The hall of famer took only 114 putts over 72 holes with 31 one-putts and just one three-putt during the four rounds.

Casper edged out Winged Foot pros Claude Harmon and Mike Souchak, who finished tied for third. Local favorite Doug Ford tied for fifth with Arnold Palmer. Ford was a perennial winner in Westchester, taking the 1956 Met Open title as well as four Met PGA Championships, three Westchester PGAs, and the Westchester Open in 1961 and '63. When he won the Met Open in 1956, Ford was at Putnam CC and, after stints at Tam O'Shanter and Vernon Hills, wound up his career as the head professional at the Spook Rock Golf Course when it first opened in the late 60's.

Also in 1959, Charlie Sifford, the pioneering African-American golfer, played at Winged Foot in his first major championship, finishing in 32nd place two years before the PGA of America allowed African-Americans to play on the PGA Tour.

Amateur Jack Nicklaus, 19, played in his third straight US Open in 1959, but missed the cut for the second time with two rounds of 77. After 1959, Nicklaus made 25 consecutive cuts at the US Open, through 1984, also at Winged Foot.

1974 - Hale Irwin captured the 1974 US Open championship by surviving what is considered the most difficult event in the tournament's history. The penal rough, narrow fairways, and slick greens practically eliminated birdies and not a single player broke par in the first round. Irwin won with a total score of 287, seven over par. His win was two strokes ahead of the battered field. The tournament became known as "The Massacre at Winged Foot."

A young pro named John Buzcek, who had won the 1970 Westchester Open when he was an assistant pro at Winged Foot, was in the top 10 for the first two rounds of the 1974 US Open. His 83-73 over the weekend led to a T-35 finish. Much later in his career, he would return to the county as Winged Foot's sixth head professional from 2006 to 2009.

1984 - Winged Foot's fourth US Open was again decided in a playoff, this one won by Fuzzy Zoeller over Greg Norman. In regulation play, Zoeller led Norman by three shots after the turn, but Norman evened the score by the time he reached eighteen. He airmailed his approach shot into the grandstand but saved par by taking a penalty-free drop and holing a 45-foot putt. Zoeller, who was waiting to play from the eighteenth fairway, thought he needed a birdie to win and waved a jesting white towel in surrender before making a par to force a playoff. Zoeller wiped up Norman the next day, posting a 67 to win by eight strokes. Norman waved his own white towel on eighteen.

2006 - The 2006 US Open will forever be known not for who won, but for who lost. In one of the wildest finales in tournament history, Phil Mickelson collapsed on the eighteenth hole. Often overlooked is the fact that Jim Furyk and Colin Montgomerie did the same, although not in quite as dramatic fashion. Mickelson missed the fairway off the tee, clipped a tree, plugged into a greenside bunker and double-bogeyed the hole to plunge into a three-way tie for second. Furyk missed a five foot putt for par on eighteen, while Montgomerie left his approach shot short and in the right rough, then followed that with three putts on the difficult green. The result was a one-stroke victory by Geoff Ogilvy, who notched his only major title with the win.

2020 - Bryson DeChambeau overpowered the West Course and the field to win by six strokes in a championship tournament made strange by Covid's impact and the lack of on-site spectators. DeChambeau dominated with both power and finesse. He hit only 23 fairways for the week, but was so long off the tee that he was able to blast out of the wicked rough with a surprising amount of finesse to set up makable putts.

A Winged Foot Century of Other Championships

1940 US Amateur – Dick Chapman, a WFGC member and winner of the 1951 British Amateur, dominated the final round with an 11 and 9 win over W.B. McCullough.

1949 Walker Cup – won by the US team 10 and 2 under captain Francis Ouimet. The team included local favorite Willie Turnesa.

1957 US Women's Open – Betsy Rawls was awarded the trophy after Jackie Pung mistakenly signed an incorrect scorecard and was disqualified. Winged Foot members felt so bad for Pung they took up a collection for her that totaled $3,000, more than the purse she lost.

1972 US Women's Open – Susie Maxwell Berning won on the East Course, the second of her three US Women's Open titles.

1980 US Senior Open – Roberto De Vicenzo won the first edition of this major championship. The Argentinian won 229 professional tournaments worldwide but is best remembered for signing an incorrect scorecard in the 1968 Masters that kept him out of a playoff for the title.

1997 PGA Championship – Davis Love III won his only major under a perfectly-timed rainbow that appeared over the eighteenth green as he sank the winning putt.

2004 US Amateur – Ryan Moore won the championship in the same year he won the NCAA Individual Championship, the US Amateur Public Links, and the Western Amateur.

2016 US Amateur Four-Ball – SMU teammates Ben Baxter & Andrew Buchanan won in the second year this championship was played.

Notable Holes

Winged Foot West #10

#10 West, 194 yards, par 3 – (2020) Billy Casper only three-putted once during the 1959 championship and his bobble came on the treacherous tenth hole, which A.W. Tillinghast named the finest par three he ever designed. When Davis Love III won the PGA Championship on the course in 1997, he said this hole is "perhaps the hardest par three we play that doesn't have water on it." The hole doesn't need water—deep, steep-faced bunkers flank the green and the putting surface is so narrow that sand saves are essentially impossible. You can't run the ball onto the green from the tee, either, since the narrow throat in front is crowned so a ball landing there will kick—where else?—into a bunker. Even a safe shot to the green doesn't guarantee a par—just ask Billy Casper.

#1 West, 451 yards, par 4 - (2020) The West makes a statement on the first hole: every shot counts on this course. "Our opening hole is long and the green is brutal," says WFGC head pro Mike Gilmore. "It's hard enough getting there—you've got a long poke to begin with. Then you have all you can do just to keep it on the green. Above the hole is impossible. If you can two-putt that green, you're off to a great start."

#3 West, 243 yards, par 3 - (2020) There may be a time and place to go pin-hunting, but the third hole during the US Open isn't either one because, even for the pros, it's a long shot to a tiny target. "The narrow opening to the green is visually intimidating," Gilmore says. "And you should be intimidated! If you don't hit the green, your chances of getting up and down are nil. If you land in one of the bunkers on either side of the green, you've got a problem because the green runs away from both of them. Even if you hit the green from the tee, it's not an easy two-putt." That's why Billy Casper laid up off the tee to the front of the green, chipped on, and putted for par every day in 1959.

#14 West, 452 yards, par 4 – (2021) It is difficult to choose the best new hole on Winged Foot, so we turned to US Open scores to aid the decision. In 2006, the fourteenth hole was the third most difficult of the tournament, a rank that held up in 2020 when it's scoring average of 4.3 made it the fourth toughest, according to longtime WFGC member Gene Westmoreland. Major alterations to the green complex as part of the Gil Hanse restoration changed the nature of the hole in several meaningful ways. The green itself was expanded back to its original size and shamrock shape. The greenside bunkers, which weren't part of the original design, were removed and a cross bunker restored short of the green on the left. Removal of trees behind the green was another major change that significantly altered your depth perception when planning your second shot.

Winged Foot West #9

#9 West, 513 yards, par 5 - (2022) Nine West offers perhaps the best view on the entire property of the iconic Winged Foot clubhouse. It's a heck of a golf hole, too. Tillinghast described it as one of the toughest holes on the course and Gil Hanse's restoration of what he called a "wedge green" brought new perimeter pin positions into play.

#17 West, 435 yards, par 4 - (2015) "It's best to favor the left side of the fairway off the tee," says head pro Mike Gilmore. "The right side has bunkers and trees." The fairway on the seventeenth hole isn't wide, though, so straight is good, especially for a bogey golfer who doesn't want to try to hit a perfect three-wood out of the rough on his second shot. The real test on the hole comes with the approach, though. Gilmore points out, "The green is very narrow for a long hole and has bunkers on both sides. Missing it pin high is a very tough up and down." Gilmore suggests playing it smart may be the bogey golfer's best chance for a small number. "To ensure no worse than bogey it may be best to hit your approach shot just to the front of the green." That leaves you with a straightforward, generally uphill chip.

#18 West, 430 yards, par 4 - (2026) The final hole on Winged Foot's West Course has been the scene of numerous triumphs and tragedies (remember Phil Mickelson's debacle?), but one stroke on the treacherous green in 1929 put Westchester County on the world's golf map with a star. It was the final hole of regulation in the US Open, and amateur Bobby Jones faced a must-make 12-foot downhill, sidehill putt to tie Al Espinosa and force a playoff. The hole was cut near the center of the green and most players would expect it to break to the right since the green slopes predominantly from back to front. For this putt, though, there's a double break, ending with a very slight turn to the left away from the peak of the green's steep false front. Jones saw it, sank the putt, and secured his third US Open championship in a 36-hole playoff the next day.

#7 East, 471 yards, par 4 - (2010) A.W. Tillinghast named this hole "Quaker" not, I suspect, because it is gentle and peace-loving but rather due to the feeling you'll get in your knees trying to make a par. The hole lies fairly straight away off the tee, but driving anywhere but to the right side will send your ball down the left-sloping fairway and into the trees or, if you really bang a drive, into the 35-yard-long bunker guarding that side. Keep in mind that the drive is the easiest shot you'll have on this hole! There is more sand than grass around the long, narrow green, so choose the right weapon for your assault on the flag. The highly-contoured green doesn't really have an "easy" pin position, either, so expect a little more knee knocking before your ball finds the bottom of the cup. If our imaginary course were rated, this would probably be the number one handicap hole on the scorecard.

#17 East, 227 yards, par 3 - (2016) The toughest hole during last year's Met Open played on Winged Foot's East course was the brutal par three seventeenth hole, a long par three with a tiny green. It played to a stroke average of 3.7 during the tournament—extremely high considering it's the only hole on the course without a bunker. The difficulty is the target, which is small and protected by a massive grass depression on the left side. Most players would rather play out of nicely predictable sand than have their ball snuggled down into grass where the outcome is in doubt. Putting on this green is no cinch either; Tillinghast named it "Lightnin'" for a reason.

#6 East, 196 yards, par 3 - (2019) The sixth hole on Winged Foot's East Course has a very apt name: "Trouble." For a par three, it's remarkable how much trouble A.W. Tillinghast built into this one golf hole. From the tee, you see three greenside bunkers as well as a fairway bunker that serves no purpose other than to plant some fear into your swing thoughts. At 196 yards, it's a long hole—but it plays uphill, so you'll need an extra club. And there's a false front on the green, too, so you might want an extra club and a half. About the only break you get is the backstop on the green, which slopes back to front—although that also means you need to stop the ball quickly or you'll be putting from above the hole.

#12 East, 546 yards, par 5 - (2025) A.W. Tillinghast aptly named this hole "Long John," although there's much more required to make par than smacking a massive drive. Before you pull your longest fairway wood for your second shot, give great thought to the distance you want for your third. The front of the green is protected by a wicked bunker, so you may not want a half-wedge in if you're not comfortable with less than a full swing.

WYKAGYL COUNTRY CLUB
NEW ROCHELLE

Wykagyl #9 (played as #18 in Westchester Open)

Wykagyl Country Club dates its founding to 1898 when its home was a nine-hole course in Pelham. When the club lost its lease in 1904, it purchased the present site in New Rochelle and directed club member Lawrence Van Etten to design an eighteen-hole course. After World War I, Donald Ross was called in to revise the front nine. A.W. Tillinghast put his mark on the course a few years later and the current layout debuted in 1931.

A major renovation of the course was done in 2006 by Coore & Crenshaw. Numerous trees were removed, bunkering updated, and several greens recontoured. The golf course winds over hilly terrain with no parallel fairways. It is unusual in having five par fives and five par threes.

The club occupies an important chapter in the annals of professional golf history. The organizational meeting of the Professional Golfers Association was held in 1916. The meeting was called by Rodman Wanamaker (who donated the PGA Championship trophy that bears his name) and the organization's first president was Robert White, Wykagyl's Head Golf Professional from 1922 through 1926.

Wykagyl has hosted numerous tournaments of the first order, including the Palm Beach Round Robin seven times from 1948 to 1957, the Ike Championship in 2013, and the Met Open in 2018. The LPGA made Wykagyl its New York metro home as early as 1977, staging the JAL Big Apple Classic and the LPGA Sybase Classic from 1990 to 2006 and the HSBC Women's World Match Play in 2007. In 2017, Wykagyl hosted the Westchester Open.

Notable Holes

Wykagyl #15 (JF)

#15, 341 yards, par 4 - (2023) "The fifteenth hole at Wykagyl may be short, but it is no walk in the park," says director of instruction Anna Ausanio. "When I step onto the tee, I play a conservative shot using either a hybrid or fairway wood to give me comfortable yardage to the green. My most crucial move while making that swing is to allow my arms to start first from the top of the backswing back down to the ball. This produces a nice, high, baby draw. My worst mistake is trying to overpower my shot and not being patient, causing me to come over the top." She points out that the hole's green is very tricky, too, with multiple tiers and a false front, so choose a layup distance where you can hit a wedge you believe in.

Wykagyl #11 (JF)

#11, 161 yards, par 3 - (2024) "This is a beautifully intimidating hole," according to Patrick Schwarze, first assistant pro at the club. "It plays 10 yards less than the distance downhill, but that can change with the wind. The green is really small, so aim for the middle and commit to your swing."

#9, 500 yards, par 5 - (2008) Wykagyl Country Club opened an almost-new golf course in 2007, the result of a massive overhaul that altered the character of nearly every hole. One of the biggest changes was on the ninth, a formerly tight, almost restrictive, par five. When the architects removed dozens of trees on the hole, they might as well have hired a skywriter to trace "GO FOR IT" across the sky above the clubhouse. It's now a true risk and reward hole, according to head pro Ben Hoffhine, because "you now have the option of going for the green in two. You just have to steer clear of the deep bunkers guarding the green." Those bunkers aren't just next to the green, either. They stretch back about a hundred yards along the left side of the fairway just waiting to swallow up a risk-taker's mis-guided ball.

#18, 422 yards, par 4 - (2011) What makes a good finishing hole? To me, it should be a difficult par but not an impossible birdie hole, one where a match leader has to think twice before settling for par against a charging contender. That's the eighteenth hole at Wykagyl, which offers anyone who hits two strong, straight shots a birdie putt. Anything less, though, and a big number can hit the scorecard, as can be attested by LPGA legend

Annika Sorenstam who needed three approach attempts to hold a shot on the steeply elevated green in the 2006 Sybase Classic. On the opposite side of the question, the elevated green presents another challenge—one experienced by *Westchester Magazine* publisher Ralph Martinelli. The green's surface is blind from the fairway, so Ralph didn't see his ball find the cup for an eagle.

#7, 171 yards, par 3 - (2015) One of the county's most challenging par threes, Wykagyl's seventh hole has a severely sloped green from back left to front right. Multiple bunkers surround the hole and play from the tee is over a deep, intimidating valley. Head pro Ben Hoffine says par is possible, even for the bogey golfer. "Hitting the green is a big plus but any tee shot right of the green still gives the golfer an opportunity to make three," he says. "Any kind of chip, pitch or bunker shot from the left will be nearly impossible to keep on the green. Because of the severe slope, from a strategic standpoint it is always better to be right so your second shot is uphill." Hoffine recommends managing your expectations. "Wykagyl is unique in that it has five par three holes," he says. "If a bogey golfer can walk away from them with five bogeys they will have a good chance of posting a good score."

 # 10, 513 yards, par 5 - (2020) How can such a short par five be rated as the number-two handicap hole at a course as complex as Wykagyl? The answer is simple, according to head pro John Deigan. "A good drive sets up the possibility of reaching this green in two," he says, "but you must avoid the bunkers left of the elevated green at all costs. They're deep and don't leave you much green to work with. The safer strategy is to lay back to your favorite wedge distance on the second shot. Be sure to check the pin position on the deep three-tier green, though, before you choose the club for that crucial third shot."

GOLF BEFORE AND AFTER THE PANDEMIC

The Business of Golf in Westchester (2014)

Anyone who's tried to play the game of golf knows it's hard. The business of golf is hard, too, and it's not getting any easier as the golfing population ages and new players become more and more difficult to attract. "The biggest issue facing the industry overall is the decline in membership at private clubs," says Bob Thomas, executive director of the Westchester Golf Association (WGA) and the Caddie Scholarship Fund. "The cost of keeping the doors open continually increases and it's a challenge to keep the number of members high enough so that cash-flow is sufficient to maintain the clubs."

The ups and downs of the economy impact golf just like they do every other business that's dependent on discretionary spending. But the real threats to the game's health are the lifestyle changes that send Dad to junior's soccer game instead of to the golf course on Saturday morning, and Mom to her office instead of to the country club on Wednesday afternoon. The survival of the golf business in Westchester—just as in the rest of the country—depends on how well the club owners adapt to the changing world around them.

Heath Wassem, president of the PGA Metropolitan Section (Met PGA), which represents golf professionals in the New York metro area, explains the difficulties: "The baby boomers were expected to flock to the game when they hit their 50s and 60s, when they had more free time and disposable income," he says. "But they haven't. Private clubs are finding it harder to replace the normal attrition of members each year."

If you're not a country-club golfer, of course, you might ask, "Who cares?" The answer is summed up nicely by Jay Mottola, executive director of the Metropolitan Golf Association (MGA), which represents 565 golf clubs (public and private) with 140,000 members in the New York metro area: "Golf is a huge economic engine for Westchester. The employment numbers alone are important."

There is public golf here, but the economic dynamo of the golf business in Westchester is driven by the members-only and very private country clubs. Of the 51 golf clubs in the county, 38 are private and available for play only to members and their guests. Of the 13 others, six are operated by the Westchester County parks Department and open to everyone; four are semi-private courses that give preference to residents of the communities who own them; and three are privately owned daily-fee courses open to the public. Of the 38 private clubs, 30 are owned by the members and operate on a not-for-profit basis. The other eight courses are owned by investors—including the eponymous Trump National Golf Club in Briarcliff Manor. Also contributing to the county's golf business are driving ranges, golf retailers, and various golf instruction businesses that serve particular niches in the market.

Tallying Golf's Impact

Just how big is the golf business in Westchester? Even though the private clubs are generally reluctant to share the details of their financial statements, the not-for-profit member-owned clubs file publicly available tax returns, so estimating the size of the golf business in the county can be based on more than speculation. Using that data for 2011 (the last year available) for 27 clubs and projecting it to the 38 total clubs, we estimate that the private clubs in the county generate revenues of $289 million annually. Add in the county-owned courses ($9.5 million in projected revenue, according to 2013 budget figures), and you've got a nearly $300-million industry—and that's not including revenue from the other segments of the golf business.

Applying the same methods (and sources) to employment data reveals that an estimated 5,600 people are employed in various positions in the golf business in Westchester—not counting the 1,500 men and women who work as caddies, who are independent contractors. About 50 percent of the county's golf positions are seasonal, but the estimated 7,100-worker total puts golf on par with the retail clothing business and real estate sector in the county. These golf professionals serve some 90,000 golfers, an estimate arrived at by applying the national percentage of golfers to Westchester County's population.

Those numbers are large enough to matter. There are a few other numbers that count, too. Because the majority of the clubs are not-for-profit, nearly every dime of the $289 million they take in is spent in the county. According to the MGA's 2013 Cooperative Golf Club Survey of member clubs in Westchester and Fairfield Counties, the average club had net income of just $107,000 after expenses. Payrolls at the private clubs amount to an estimated $142 million and, while not many of them pay income taxes (on what income?), they certainly pay property taxes—about $319,000 per club, or roughly $13.4 million for the 42 clubs not owned by the county or municipalities. The clubs also generated $15.7 million for charities through outings last year, too, according to the MGA.

Clearly, a sharp, sudden decline in a business of that size would certainly affect the county economy. The industry's prospects are mixed, according to Ken Wang, owner of Pound Ridge Golf Club, the newest golf course in Westchester. "The muni courses are always going to be fine, just as Winged Foot and Quaker Ridge will always be fine," he says. "Like in most industries, though, the middle of the market tends to get killed." There could indeed be casualties in the golf business if the private clubs and daily-fee operators stick their heads in the sand and hope the problems go away. While there are some with grit in their hair, many golf clubs are improving their product, inventing new models of business, and fighting for growth.

Finding the Sweet Spot

Knollwood Country Club, the second—oldest golf club in the county, is one of the more aggressive member-owned clubs. "We've concentrated over the last eighteen months on improving our amenities with a significant upgrade program to enhance the experience of our existing members and, hopefully, attract some new ones," says Knollwood President Bob Hughes, citing upgrades to both the clubhouse and golf course. "The most prominent change was strengthening and lengthening our eighteenth hole." He's not daunted by rising and falling membership numbers. "Cycles happen and you adapt to them," he says. "We're coming up on our 120th year, which is something very few businesses can say."

Jeffrey Mendell and his partners are pursuing a completely different business model. Mendell is managing partner of the investment group that acquired an existing course and opened Brynwood Golf & Country Club in Armonk in 2010. "We entered the business during the financial crisis," he explains, "and we tried to create something that didn't exist. Westchester is blessed with a lot of great golf courses that cater to the high end, so we created a club that appeals to a broader section of the market. We priced it aggressively and we've attracted a cross section of people from all walks of life."

Brynwood did away with heavy initiation fees, created annual membership packages to fit the lifestyles of different demographics, and brought in Troon Golf to manage the facility. "Being an investor-owned club, we're trying to make money at this business," Mendell says. "It's hard to do. When we get into phase two, we will improve on that."

The next phase, which has been tied up in the Town of Armonk's rezoning process, includes constructing 88 luxury townhouses along part of the property, building an entirely new clubhouse, and the redesign of the golf course by "US Open doctor" Rees Jones. The end result will be a resort-style golf community unlike anything in the county. Mendell says he expects the regulatory hurdles to be surmounted this year. (A similar struggle is going on between the Town of Mamaroneck and the owners of Hampshire Country Club.)

Ken Wang is taking yet another approach. His Pound Ridge Golf Club is a decidedly upscale facility with a $40-million course designed by Pete Dye, arguably America's leading golf architect. Pound Ridge occupies a unique place in the Westchester market as a totally public course offering top-quality golf on a daily-fee basis. The facility couldn't have opened at a worse time—2008—as far as the economic outlook goes. "Our growth curve has the right shape, but it's taking a little longer than we would have liked," Wang says. "Last year, rounds played were up, although not as much as we wanted because the weather was so poor in the spring."

Wang believes he can appeal to middle- and high-income golfers who can afford but aren't interested in the country-club lifestyle for various reasons. "In the old days, people joined private clubs at a certain stage in their lives," he says. "They had kids, and they spent the day at the club, playing golf, then cards, while the kids were at the pool, then they stayed for dinner. That model is clearly shot." There's a cost factor, too, according to Wang. "The economics of country-club golf are well known. It's going to cost you around $1,000 per round unless you play a lot of golf. We're around $195 per round, and even less on weekdays."

Appealing to the family market is the tack adopted by other clubs, too. Eugene Donovan, a long-time member at Bonnie Briar Country Club in Larchmont, believes the club has been successful because it is promoted to (and priced to fit the budget of) young golfers with kids. "We made the assumption that the attraction would be the golf course instead of the clubhouse, so we put a large percentage of our money into the course," he explains. "We're still making improvements to it."

Broadening the Appeal (and the Business)

While many (but certainly not enough) of the private clubs, like Bonnie Briar, have active junior programs, one of the biggest obstacles to growing golf in Westchester is the dearth of entry points for other kids into the game. Most of the private clubs are restricted to members' children and perhaps a few of their guests.

One effort to introduce kids to golf is The First Tee program, whose metropolitan chapter was founded with help from the MGA and Met PGA at Mosholu Golf Course in the Bronx. Some 530 children, many from Westchester, participate each year at Mosholu and the program will be offered at Westchester Golf Range in White Plains beginning this year.

The county-owned courses and public driving ranges offer kids' programs, too, but opportunities to actually play the game on a golf course are limited. The county courses allow kids under 13 on the course only when accompanied by an adult, and then only with the permission of the golf pro.

Another market that's not been very well served in Westchester (or nationally) is new women golfers. The Women's Metropolitan Golf Association (WMGA) promotes the sport, mostly among the private clubs, but opportunities for women who want to learn the game are somewhat limited. One organization that makes a serious effort to bring women into golf is the Westchester chapter of the Executive Women's Golf Association (EWGA), which has about 250 members.

"As a way to get more women involved in the game, we have clinics and educational opportunities specifically designed for rookies and beginners," explains EWGA Westchester President Hollie West. "We have a rookie league each year where new players go out with a more experienced player. It's not really about golf lessons as much as it is about etiquette and getting around the course.

Despite weak local efforts to grow the number of golfers in Westchester, accounts of the decline of golf are like reports of Mark Twain's death—greatly exaggerated. The country clubs may be fighting for members and under-served markets aren't being tapped, but the business overall seems to be holding its own against an uncertain economy and the demographic shifts working against it.

The number of rounds played at the county-owned courses remained essentially flat (minus one percent) from 2003 to 2012, although it was down in 2013 due to bad weather throughout the peak spring season. Membership in the private clubs has leveled out in the last two years, according to the MGA survey, with 41 percent of Westchester clubs reporting an increase and 44 percent a decrease.

Nationally, more golf clubs have closed than opened in recent years, according to the 2011 Golf Economy Report by the National Golf Foundation, but the opposite is true in Westchester, says Charlie Robson, executive director of the Met PGA. "If you look at the past 20 years, we've added some excellent upscale facilities," he notes. During that period, Ridgeway Country Club in White Plains closed, while hundreds of millions of dollars were invested in new clubs like Hudson National Golf Club in Croton-on-Hudson, Anglebrook Golf Club in Lincolndale, Hollow Brook Golf Club in Cortlandt Manor, the county-owned Hudson Hills Golf Course in Ossining, and Pound Ridge Golf Club. New courses were built over existing ones by GlenArbor Golf Club in Bedford and Trump National in Briarcliff Manor.

Robson also points out that employment in the metropolitan area—at least for the golf professionals who run the courses, give the lessons, and manage the retail operations in the clubs—has increased. "In 1997, we had 461 PGA members and 145 in the apprentice program. In 2013, we had 677 PGA members and 76 in the apprentice program," he says. "The increase not only reflects the number of facilities added but illustrates two other facts—that clubs and daily-fee courses hired more professionals to provide a higher level of service, and that a number of new golf teaching and retail facilities have opened." Those include companies like GolfTEC and Dick's Sporting Goods, which hire PGA pros to provide expert advice and instruction to customers.

The future of golf in Westchester? "I don't see anything changing quickly or dramatically," says MGA's Mottola. "Some of the initiatives and efforts to attract members will help local clubs do well. Some of the lower-echelon clubs may develop into hybrids of private and semi-private clubs. Every single club has really analyzed their operational costs and cut unneeded spending. That's helped get them through the tough economic times. Long-term, that will bode well for the clubs."

The State of the Game in Westchester (2017)

Like a perfect storm, new leaders were chosen in the past year for the three organizations powering golf in our area. We gathered the new management of the MGA, the Met PGA, and the WMGA for a roundtable discussion of the future of the game.

Who's Who?

The Metropolitan Golf Association (MGA) represents more than 140,000 golfers in 520 member clubs in the NY Metro area. It stages 19 championships including the Met Open, maintains the GHIN handicap system, and provides a myriad of other services to local golfers and golf clubs.

Michael Sullivan, President, MGA – Sullivan is the 63rd president in the association's history. He's been on the Executive Committee since 2010 and served as treasurer and vice president as well as president of the Long Island Golf Association.

Brian Mahoney, Executive Director, MGA – Mahoney was most recently Director of Rules and Competitions for the MGA until he assumed the helm. He began with the organization as an intern while in college.

The Metropolitan Section of the PGA of America (Met PGA) represents over 800 golf professionals in the area. These club pros manage golf course operations and teach the game to players at all levels. Among many other functions, the Met PGA conducts tournaments and manages the PGA Junior Tour.

Brian Crowell, President, Met PGA – Crowell, a longtime PGA member, has served as head professional at Leewood GC, GlenArbor GC, and currently is Director of Golf at Silo Ridge Field Club.

Jeff Voorheis, Executive Director, Met PGA – Voorheis had served as tournament director of the section before he became Executive Director. He came to the Met PGA in 2004 after working in sports marketing.

The Women's Metropolitan Golf Association (WMGA) is the second oldest golf association for women in the US and conducts 30 competitions each year for its 180 member clubs and 2,400 individual members.

Sarah Relyea, Director of Operations, WMGA – Relyea, a standout amateur golfer in New Jersey, served as tournament director for the WMGA before moving up to the top position this year.

Cheryl Brayman, President, WMGA – Brayman, a longtime board member, served as a director representing Long Island on the WMGA board before her election to her current position.

The Roundtable

Donelson What's the state of golf in Westchester and the Hudson Valley?

Mahoney "Westchester County is unique versus the rest of the golf world. It has great golf history architecturally and culturally, so our message is extremely positive about the game both private and public. Thirty percent of our Westchester clubs have wait lists for membership. That's a very healthy, positive number that speaks volumes about the appetite for the game of golf in the county."

Voorheis "Westchester is as close to bullet proof as you can get when it comes to economics. There will always be that group of clubs here that will have a waiting list until the end of time. But there will also be those other tiers that have to re-invent themselves. We've seen many of them do that. They build practice facilities and other amenities. They give the customer what they want."

Relyea "It's an exciting time for women. You're seeing highly competitive, skilled golfers and more women are playing at all levels."

Brayman "We put out 1,200 women for five team matches over two and a half weeks every spring. That's absolutely phenomenal."

Sullivan "The economy and behavior changes so rounds played may be down but participation is up. Our traditional player who now plays 52 rounds a year might have played 70 in the past. Now, they're going to the club to chip and putt, take a lesson, hit balls on the range over their lunch hour, but may not be playing as many rounds. The resources needed to serve that member are the same. Someone has to get their bag from the bag room, put it on a cart, set up the range, give them a lesson, maintain the putting green, and fix their lunch so they can go back to work."

Crowell "On a national level, you hear about the challenges faced by other places but we are lucky. We are in a special little zone where everyone really appreciates the traditions of golf and so many clubs are safe here."

Donelson Does that mean we're standing still?

Voorheis "Even in this safe haven where we operate, there are a number of clubs that aren't doing as well as they would like. The challenge is to marry that tradition we revere with what the next generation wants. We may cringe at the idea of music in the golf cart or turning the formal club dining room into a bar and grill with TVs and chicken wings, but if that's what the next generation is looking for, we better find a way to marry that to our traditions."

Crowell "Just as clubs are reinventing themselves, PGA pros have to reinvent themselves. We have to look beyond the traditional methods of entertainment to how many different levels of excitement can be created for families. Golf is just one way. Ultimately, we're measured as PGA pros by the volume of activity at the club because all of that leads to a great experience and a healthy club bottom line."

Mahoney "Clubs are reevaluating their business plans. You see more openness to junior memberships, to summer memberships, and they're bringing on membership directors, someone who is proactively trying to engage new generations of golfers. One of my favorite sayings is, 'Don't let tradition get in the way of evolution.' There are some members who want it one way and don't want to change, but the world is changing and if you don't change with it you can be left behind."

"For example, the MGA Men's four ball championship will be held for the first time in conjunction with our Women's four ball this year just as the USGA held the Men's and Women's Open Championships at Pinehurst. The men will play Westchester Country Club's West Course at the same time the women compete on the South Course."

Crowell "It's got to be less about the score and more about the experience. We have to keep working on nine-hole member guests, or more twilight events, or more family events, six-hole rounds, three holes during lunch. We've got to find ways to make golf wider than a narrow eighteen-hole stroke-play round."

Sullivan "Or how about a Saturday member/guest like I played in last year at Ardsley? What a great idea!"

Donelson It sounds like there's a revolution in the works

Mahoney "Engaging new golfers is our biggest issue. Consider the absolute newbie player, for example. He or she has no interest in standing on the first tee and having a bunch of hecklers watch them shank a few shots. They're much more open to a concept like Top Golf where they can just hit balls and enjoy golf in a totally different environment. Or consider kids who engage with the game virtually through a simulator or video games."

Sullivan "It's all about the experience. Everyone is worried about cell phones and jeans taking away from the traditions of the game but I think the opposite is true. The more people you have in the game, the more that will come to embrace the traditions. If you turn them away at the beginning, you have no chance to build a feeder system."

Voorheis "Speaking of technology, look at all the phones around this table. We've seen vendors who have come up with some creative apps where kids can marry golf with social media. The concept is that utilizing an app to create a community could encourage more kids to play and current players to play more."

Mahoney "We are committed financially and philosophically to some technology initiatives that will come out in the short term. I had an interesting experience at the USGA Junior Girls Championship at Nassau Country Club last year. I came into the lunchroom and every single girl was on their phone checking what the outcome of that round did to their AJGA rankings. The MGA will continue to invest in mobile social technology as a means to attract and connect with golfers."

Crowell "The club that doesn't let you take a cell phone on the golf course today—they're gone. Being rude is one thing, but let the phones get out there. Let the kids have fun. Let the grownups have fun!"

Donelson What are your organizations doing to grow the game?

Brayman "The WMGA has been a private club association, but we are considering opening our membership to independent members so they can play in our tournaments. We are also trying to encourage our B players to participate more in our tournaments, so we've instituted a B player of the year award. We get a tremendous amount of interest in our team matches in the early spring but participation wanes somewhat after that."

Relyea "The association is changing with the times. Girls To the Tee is held at Westchester Country Club twice in the season. We get about 125

girls ages 6 to 18 raring to go. They're all skill levels from first timers who may not even have a set of clubs to juniors who take lessons twice a week from the finest professionals in the area."

Crowell "We have over 1,300 kids in our Junior Tour programs. We are constantly looking for ways to run more tournaments to accommodate them. It's a great problem to have. Now you also have PGA Junior League and Drive, Chip & Putt. Those two programs have been home runs. The PGA Junior League with the jerseys and the scramble format is getting a whole different level of excitement into golf."

Sullivan "The Golfworks program is something we're really proud of. It provides meaningful employment in a friendly environment for under-privileged and minority youth. We had 277 participants last year at 70 clubs. Program hours for the number of kids working was up 33% since 2014 to 62,700 hours. When you add the caddie scholarship programs and the First Tee, it all adds up to bringing more kids to the game."

Voorheis "We're excited about a couple of things we're going to do this year. I'm bullish on them not being all about competitions. We do so much for competitive players, but it's important for us to have leaderboards about things other than what score they shot. It can be 'how many times did you play?' or 'how many putts did you hit?' To kids, especially in a game as difficult as golf, it's easy to get turned off."

Crowell "We have to find other ways to reward them. I'm not a fan of participation ribbons, but if you celebrate closest to the pins on the leader-board, that helps recognize more players. If there's a scramble format, a kid can make a putt and feel like a hero without shooting 72."

Sullivan "If you posted on your leaderboards not just the scores, but the kids who just shot the best round they've ever personally had, you'll be flooded with social media pictures."

Mahoney "There are levels. There's a right group for that and then there's another group with an insatiable appetite for competition and those people need different things. If we're going to get growth, we have to do something for all of them.

Donelson How can you increase participation by adults?

Mahoney "Participation in our tournaments is very strong. We're at the breaking point in terms of growth, so our focus is going to be on more collaboration and perhaps retiring some competitions that don't make as much sense in the culture today. Consider qualifiers. Let's say the Westchester Golf Association is holding their qualifier for their amateur championship and the MGA is holding one for ours. If they're both not at capacity, we could hold one qualifier together."

"To enlarge our audience, we're going to roll out some public golf leagues as a beta test this year. We have access to the USGA software that was built to manage those, so we are trying to find five public courses we will roll these out to. There is such an insatiable appetite for competition here, we can facilitate that at all levels. Many of them will be tested as nine-hole leagues that will capture more people."

Sullivan "We focus on programs like 'playing it forward' and pace of play so we are making the game more enjoyable. That will raise participation. Even with all the technology, though, the activity that still matters is going outside and swinging the club, walking the course, raking a bunker, and playing with your friends and family. It's still a physical activity and we need to keep that in mind."

Voorheis "We're so proud of what our PGA professionals have done for their communities with PGA HOPE, which stands for 'helping our patriots everywhere.' Kelli Clayton on our staff plugged into three VA hospitals in the area and connected them with some golf courses where the PGA professionals volunteer to instruct them. To be honest, golf is probably the least important part of the mix. It's all about getting out of the institution and being with somebody who asks you how your day is going and how you're feeling. One thing golf has is that moment when you're standing over a golf ball and you forget about everything except that shot."

New Golf Leaders (2019)

Golf may have some growth issues nationwide, but the new presidents of the two NY Metro golf organizations, the Metropolitan Golf Association (MGA) and the Women's Metropolitan Golf Association (WMGA), are both optimistic about the game, especially in Westchester.

As it happens, both presidents live in Rye and know the local golf scene inside and out. Lori Ann Cerullo, president of the WMGA, took up the game when she worked in sales for IBM. Today she plays in a public league at Maple Moor and belongs to the Rye Golf Club. MGA President Tod Pike got his start in the game at Rye GC and has been a long time member at the Apawamis Club in Rye.

"The MGA supports the game in a lot of different ways," Pike explains. "We share best practices between clubs and stage dozens of competitions." The MGA also runs the handicap system in this area and provides course rating services. Pike adds, "We are perhaps best known for our many tournaments. The elite golfer gets a chance to play in many of them, but our schedule has a lot of 'net' events as well, so the average golfer who wants to compete using their handicap can test themselves in a lot of different formats."

Cerullo explains that the WMGA's mission is to foster women's and girls' golf. In addition to a healthy schedule of tournaments and team matches, the organization stages introductory events like the Girls to the Tee, held at three metro locations including Westchester Country Club.

Both presidents are focused on the future of the game. "Women have jobs and kids. How do we get golf on their to-do list? How do we make it easy and fun?" Cerullo asks. "We are exploring different venues and formats and competitions. There are some women who are real competitors and others who aren't so much, but they all get into the camaraderie of the game." The WMGA has also opened its doors to independent members who may not belong to a club. Through its foundation, the group also provides fellowships for junior golfers to enable them to play in events they might not otherwise be able to afford.

"We need to ask ourselves whether we're providing avenues into the game like previous generations had," Pike observes. "We provide greater access to the game through our Play Days, which open a number of courses to the public that may not have a lot a different places to play." The MGA has also initiated league play at some daily fee courses, conducts caddie training workshops to bring young people into the game, and supports youth clinics in conjunction with the First Tee.

Golf After the Pandemic (2021)

Golf turned out to be the recreation of choice for thousands of Westchester residents in 2020, with the number of rounds played reaching record numbers at courses across the county. Are we in for more of the same this season? "The MGA eagerly anticipates the 2021 golf season with renewed enthusiasm and extreme optimism," says MGA executive director Brian Mahoney. "While courses and golfers continue to adapt to ever-changing health guidance, the reward remains a healthy 'walk in the park'. The MGA welcomes the opportunity to aid efforts to grow the game as golf is poised to reach even greater heights in 2021." The heavy schedule of tournaments staged by the MGA returns this year.

The WMGA is looking forward to the 2021 season with a full schedule of competitions, according to Executive Director Sarah Niemeier. "Our game was seen early on as a safe outlet for women to exercise and get outside with precautions in place and we will continue to keep our Covid-19 procedures in effect throughout the 2021 season. The widespread use of technology was rampant in 2020 and simple changes such as eliminating printing physical paper and posting notices electronically was such a benefit from a sustainability perspective."

"While the best golf experiences are often shotgun starts that include food and beverage, the ability for golf to be enjoyed in simpler forms was what ultimately bolstered the sport's popularity in 2020," says Met PGA executive director Jeff Voorheis. "With so much still unknown, it stands to reason that golf will enter 2021 similarly to the way it exited 2020." Voorheis believes some of the trends that emerged last year—more players carrying their own clubs and simpler food service options—may become commonplace even beyond this year.

MAJOR GOLF ORGANIZATIONS
IN WESTCHESTER

Metropolitan Golf Association
Celebrates Quasquicentennial (2022)

Golf in Westchester would not be the game we play today if a couple of dozen clubs hadn't answered the call of the greens committee at the St. Andrew's GC in Hastings-on-Hudson 125 years ago to gather at Delmonico's in Manhattan to form the Metropolitan League of Golf Clubs. We know it today as the Metropolitan Golf Association (MGA), the organization that runs our tournaments, manages our handicaps, and ensures that golf in the county and the rest of the metro area is a growing, vibrant game available to thousands of players at all levels.

When the MGA was formed in April of 1897, wooden golf tees hadn't yet been invented, much less golf carts with GPS systems. The purpose of the organization was to promote the game and arrange tournaments. The first Met Amateur Championship was held in 1899; this year's 120th edition will be contested at Fenway GC in Scarsdale. The Met Open, considered a major until WWII, premiered in 1905. Today, the MGA conducts dozens of tournaments on its own roster as well as those of affiliated groups, including the Westchester and Long Island Golf Associations, not to mention the qualifying tournaments for USGA events, like the US Open.

But the MGA has grown into much more than an operator of golf tournaments, as important as that role may be. It also rates courses, an integral but seldom-understood part of the handicap system, runs programs like Youth on Course, MGA Play Days, and numerous educational events. Then there's the MGA Foundation, which funds important efforts, like GOLFWORKS, which provides internships for hundreds of young people throughout the metro area.

Today's MGA serves every facet of the game from its headquarters in Elmsford. Membership has grown from the original 26 clubs to 520 private and public golf clubs and courses, with more than 140,000 golfers throughout the metro area.

WMGA Celebrates 125 Years of Service (2024)

Since its founding in 1899, the Women's Metropolitan Golf Association has never averted its eyes from its mission to foster women's participation in the game. This year, the WMGA celebrates its 125th anniversary with special tournaments at many of the founding clubs, an enthusiastic embrace of fun and camaraderie on the course, and an ever-stronger emphasis on bringing girls into the game.

"From clinics to college scholarships, the WMGA is all-in on girls' golf," says LPGA star and golf broadcaster Dottie Pepper.

The association, the second oldest women's golf group in America, has a proud history of achievements. One of the earliest WMGA members was Westchester-born Beatrix Hoyt, the first winner of the US Women's Amateur Championship, who took home the trophy for three consecutive years, the last of which was from Ardsley CC in 1898. Another member, Helen Hicks, began winning WMGA events as a teenager in the 1920s and was the first WMGA member to turn professional. She became one of the founding members of the LPGA in 1950.

Today, the WMGA has about 2,400 members and 180 member clubs in the metro area. The association holds some 30 tournaments and other events throughout the year, beginning with extraordinarily popular team matches where over 800 women compete to start their season in the spring.

A highlight of this year's schedule is the 120th WMGA Match Play Championship, which will be held at Ardsley CC, one of the original 23 founding clubs. Ardsley member Amy Bender won the event in 2022 and was runner-up last year to Tiya Chowdary.

Also receiving extra emphasis this year is the WMGA Foundation's college scholarship program, which has awarded over $1 million to nearly 200 girls to aid their college careers. "Our scholarships have been really well-funded the last few years," Says WMGA Executive Director Sarah Niemeier. "We're very excited to help girls go to college, especially those who are outside the private club universe because it's based on financial need."

PGA of America Metropolitan Section (Met PGA)

The PGA of America was born here in 1916, the brainchild of Wykagyl golf pro Robert White with the encouragement of business leader Rodman Wannamaker. Its purpose then, as now, was to recognize and elevate golf professionals for their contribution to the game. Today, the organization has over 28,000 members nationwide.

The Metropolitan Section has been at the forefront of the PGA of America since its founding. The organization is divided into 41 geographical sections across the United States and Met PGA has provided leadership among its national counterparts. The club professionals make the game better for everyone who plays by providing lessons and running the day-to-day operations of the golf courses they manage. Additionally, numerous programs of the Met PGA promote goodwill and growth of the game of golf. The lives of junior golfers, veterans, and those who are underserved by the game are directly impacted by the men and women of the section.

The PGA of America is perhaps best known for staging the PGA Championship, one of the four major tournaments in the sport. The first PGA Championship was held in 1916 at Siwanoy CC in Bronxville. It returned in 1923 to Pelham CC and was hosted by Winged Foot GC in 1997.

BOOKS BY DAVE DONELSON

Fiction
My Gitfiddle Summer
Hunting Elf
Heart of Diamonds
Blind Curve
Weird Golf

Nonfiction
Golf Westchester
Provence Reflections
Fathers: a Memoir
The Journal of My Seventieth Year
(four volumes)

Poetry
Cityverse & Cityverse 2
Points in Time
Visions of a Certain Age

How To
Creative Selling: Boost Your B2B Sales
The Dynamic Manager's Guides
(three volumes)

ABOUT DAVE DONELSON

Dave Donelson is a West Harrison, NY-based freelance writer, photographer, and artist with some three million words in print. In addition to golf, he has covered topics as diverse as the sex lives of American suburbanites and diamond smuggling in the Congo. His work appears regularly in dozens of national publications and he is the author and illustrator of numerous books of fiction, non-fiction, poetry, and memoir. In 2023, he was honored by the NY State Council on the Arts for *Visions of a Certain Age,* a book of graphic poetry.

Dave served on the board of the Metropolitan Golf Writers Association for twenty years in several positions including as president 2019-2020. In 2026, the association named him a recipient of the MGWA Dave Anderson Spotlight Award, given in "recognition of exemplary service by unique individuals in the golf community."

www.davedonelson.com